WEST HAM U

25 YEAR REC

SEASON BY SEASON WRITE-UPS
David Powter

EDITOR
Michael Robinson

CONTENTS

British Library Cataloguing in Publication Data
A catalogue record for this book is available from the British Library
ISBN 1-86223-010-2

Copyright © 1998;   SOCCER BOOKS LIMITED (01472-696226)
72, St. Peter's Avenue, Cleethorpes, N.E. Lincolnshire, DN35 8HU, England

Printed by Adlard Print & Typesetting Services, The Old School, The Green, Ruddington, Notts. NG11 6HH

WEST HAM UNITED
– Seasons 1973-74 to 1997-98

Despite just missing out on UEFA Cup qualification on the final day, 1997-98 was West Ham United's most successful season for twelve years. Harry Redknapp's side finished eighth and reached the quarter-final stages of both domestic cup competitions. The Hammers are now an integral part of the Premiership, having been members for five successive seasons, ending an uncomfortable phase when they yo-yoed between the top two flights.

Twenty-five years ago, West Ham had also just completed a successful season – 1972-73 – when they equalled their then best ever finish of sixth. The intervening quarter of a century has undoubtedly been the most interesting in the club's history – containing two FA Cup Final triumphs, a second European Cup Winners' Cup Final and a magnificent attempt to win the title (in 1985-86) which produced the club's best finish of third. Only five men sat in the manager's chair during those 25 years: Ron Greenwood, John Lyall, Lou Macari, Billy Bonds and Harry Redknapp. A stable situation which is quite in-keeping with the friendly East London club, whose total turnover of managers amounts to just eight this century.

Following their consistent showing the previous term, much was expected of the Hammers in 1973-74, but that optimism soon evaporated after a dismal 11 match winless start which sent them to the bottom of the table. A 1-0 win at Coventry in October stopped the rot, but it was not until 8th December that the Boleyn Ground celebrated a home win. It took a nine match unbeaten run at the turn of the year before Greenwood's men levered themselves out of relegation trouble.

Ironically, the first of those fixtures, a 4-2 home win over Norwich City on the first day of 1974, proved to be the great Bobby Moore's 544th and last League game for the club. The World Cup winning skipper donned the claret & blue once more for the first team a few days later (before moving to Fulham) when Fourth Division Hereford United visited in the third round of the FA Cup. Pat Holland's late equaliser gave the Hammers a reprieve in the East London mud, but they subsequently slid out of the competition in the replay.

The club was at its lowest ebb for many years during this transitional period. After enjoying the sophistication and subtlety of Moore, Geoff Hurst and Martin Peters, it was not easy for the fans to watch the likes of Alan Wooler and Bertie Lutton struggling to come to terms with the rudiments of the game. Fortunately, that early 1974 purple patch ensured that West Ham just avoided relegation in 18th place. New skipper Billy Bonds top scored with 13 goals and there were other important contributions from new England cap Trevor Brooking, Graham Paddon (ex-Norwich City), Mick McGiven (ex-Sunderland), the unsung Clyde Best (the second top scorer, with 12 goals) and, in his debut campaign, goalkeeper Mervyn Day.

After just two games of 1974-75 Ron Greenwood moved upstairs to take a General Manager's role and his deputy John Lyall took control of team affairs. Greenwood had been manager for more than 13 years, in which time the club captured its first two major trophies, the FA Cup and European Cup Winners' Cup, in the mid 1960s.

The Hammers sat at the bottom of the table after seven fixtures before the team started to gel. A subsequent seven match unbeaten run propelled them into the top half of the table and by Christmas they were in fifth place. However, the bubble quickly burst and they drifted to finish 13th. They won only two League games during the last third of the season due to their preoccupation with the FA Cup.

Lyall's side won through to the quarter-final with 2-1 victories over Southampton (away), Swindon Town (in an away replay) and QPR (at home). However, the footballing world only started to take them seriously after they triumphed 2-0 at a very muddy Highbury to reach the last four. The Gunners were spiked by two goal Alan Taylor – a little known bargain-buy from Rochdale. Ipswich Town had the edge in the Villa Park semi-final, but the Hammers survived to earn another tilt at Stamford Bridge. Alan Taylor again scored twice in the replay to send his side to Wembley with a 2-1 scoreline.

Ironically, West Ham's opponents in the final were Second Division Fulham (who earlier in 1974-75 knocked the Hammers out of the League Cup) – with Bobby Moore marshalling their defence. The 100,000 crowd saw the First Division side win a poor contest through two second half opportunist strikes. The two goal hero was yet again Alan Taylor, whose fairytale start to the big stage sadly also proved to be the pinnacle of his career. Lyall's first season in command was completed when Billy Bonds lifted the FA Cup skyward. The remainder of the team decked in claret & blue on 3rd May 1975 were: Day, Paddon, Brooking, Holland, John McDowell, Frank Lampard, Tommy Taylor, Kevin Lock, Billy Jennings (who was the club's top League scorer with 13 goals) and unused sub Bobby Gould.

West Ham began 1975-76 in inspired form, winning six of their first nine matches in an unbeaten run that lifted them to second place. Only two of the first 15 games were lost as the Hammers briefly topped the table in November; however, they faded throughout the remaining two-thirds of the season, scoring two goals or more in just four League games. In spite of all the early optimism they finished only 18th.

The Irons failed to win any of their last 16 League fixtures as they appeared to focus solely on Europe. Reipas Lahti (5-2 on aggregate) and Ararat Erevan (4-2 on aggregate) were knocked out at the Boleyn Ground after away draws, but further progression looked unlikely at half-time in the first leg of the quarter-final when Den Haag led 4-0. However, Jennings bagged two crucial away goals to set up a pulsating game in London. This time West Ham strode into a 3-0 lead at the break and, despite conceding one afterwards, reached the last four on away goals.

Paddon was the scorer in a 2-1 defeat in front of 60,000 at Eintracht Frankfurt in the semi-final first leg; but again the Hammers bounced back to triumph in the return. A brace from Brooking and a thunderbolt from Keith Robson made it 3-1 on the night, 4-3 on aggregate and a real 'Beer and Bubbles' night down the Barking Road.

Sadly, the passionate presence of their huge travelling support could not quite spur West Ham to repeat the 1965 success in the final, against Anderlecht, at the infamous Heysel Stadium. The Belgians eventually ran out 4-2 winners, with two of their goals coming from Francois Van der Elst – who within six years was a West Ham player. The night had started on a positive note with Holland netting the opener; however, with the help of a Lampard error and a dodgy penalty, Anderlecht triumphed despite a header from Keith Robson. Of the eleven who won the FA Cup twelve months earlier, nine started against Anderlecht. Lock had been replaced by Keith Coleman and Robson started instead of Alan Taylor. Ironically Taylor, who appeared in Brussels as a substitute, was the club's top League scorer with 13 goals.

A 4-0 defeat at Villa Park on the opening day set the pattern for 1976-77. Lyall's side spent all season struggling to climb out of the relegation zone. They entered their last game, at home to Manchester United, needing at least a draw to save their top-flight status. Despite conceding a goal within 25 seconds, West Ham finally ran out 4-2 winners on a nerve-wrecking evening to finish 17th. Bryan Robson (in his second spell at Upton Park) netted twice to finish the campaign as the top scorer on the 14 goal mark. Other 1976-77 signings who made far less impact were ex-Arsenal striker John Radford (no goals in 18 games) and wonky centre-back Bill Green. One man who was an instant success, though, was the wiry Alan Devonshire, who bolstered the midfield after joining from Non-League Southall.

The events of May 1977 only served to provide a one year stay of execution. The Hammers won only two of their first 18 games in 1977-78 and were always in relegation trouble. Three successive wins at the beginning of April raised hopes of a Houdini act, but two more defeats in their last three games signalled the end of a 20 year stay in the First Division. The Irons finished in 20th place – frustratingly only one point short of safe QPR. In his first season as a Hammer Derek Hales top scored with ten goals, one more than both David Cross (another 1977-78 signing) and Bryan Robson.

An immediate return to the top-flight looked likely as West Ham made a confident start to the 1978-79 season with a 5-2 thumping of Notts County at home and an impressive 3-0 victory at Newcastle. However, the Hammers ultimately stumbled due to a lack of consistency – they never managed to win more than two consecutive matches – especially on the road, where they were successful just six times. In the final analysis, promotion was missed by six points as they docked in fifth place. Bryan Robson was the top scorer with 24 goals. Tommy Taylor made his 340th and last League game for the Hammers in 1978-79. It was a campaign which contained two embarrassing cup defeats – to third-flight Swindon Town (at home) in the League Cup and at Fourth Division Newport County in the FA Cup.

West Ham made an abysmal start to the following campaign, losing three of their opening four games. It was not until November that their steady climb took them into the top half of the table. Promotion never looked a serious possibility – they eventually missed out by six points again in seventh place – as they got embroiled in two lengthy cup runs. Their 1979-80 League Cup hopes were finally ended by Nottingham Forest after extra-time in a fifth round replay. However, Lyall's side stuck to their task in the FA Cup. Top-flight WBA were slain 2-1 in an Upton Park replay; Orient were levered out 3-2 at Brisbane Road; and Swansea City were packed back to Wales with a 2-0 defeat to set up a sixth round clash with First Division Aston Villa. A lock-out 36,393 crowd witnessed the under-dogs dominate and deservedly triumph through Ray Stewart's second half penalty.

The Hammers looked on the ropes in the semi-final at Villa Park as Brian Kidd gave Everton the lead through a disputed penalty. However, Kidd received his marching orders after the break and Stuart Pearson equalised to take the tie to an Elland Road replay. That second game remained goalless until Devonshire scored in extra-time. The First Division side managed to equalise but, with just two minutes remaining, a rare header by Lampard sent West Ham into their second FA Cup Final in six years. The memory of the unlikely hero Lampard dancing around the corner flag will live on forever in West Ham folklore.

Another rare header – this time by the elegant Brooking – sent the FA Cup spinning across London to Newham, when a fourth First Division giant Arsenal were defeated at Wembley. That first half goal, a copious amount of industrious team-work and, most importantly, clever tactics by Lyall (who deployed a lone striker and a blanket midfield) meant that the Second Division under-dogs pulled off a richly deserved triumph. Bonzo was again able to hold the FA Cup aloft and he was followed up to the Royal Box by solid keeper Phil Parkes, Alvin Martin, 17 year-old Paul Allen (the youngest FA Cup finalist this century), Geoff Pike, Paul Brush (the unused sub), Stewart, Lampard, Devonshire (whose fine form earned him his first England cap a few weeks later), Pearson, Cross (top League scorer, with 13) and, of course, Brooking.

An opening day home defeat by Luton again raised serious doubts about West Ham's priorities in 1980-81. However, by the time the Hatters completed the double over them in November, Lyall's side looked good bets for the Championship. They had registered a 15 match unbeaten run and went on to clinch the Second Division title with a record total of 66 points – 13 more than runners-up Notts County. They lost just two further League games in the process. Only 17 men represented West Ham in that Second Division Championship campaign. Brush, Pearson, Allen, Bobby Barnes and Nicky Morgan made a handful of starts; but it was the following nucleus of 12 who really steered the Hammers back to the top-flight: Parkes, Stewart, Lampard, Bonds, Martin (who won his first England cap at the end of the campaign), Devonshire, Pike, Holland (whose career was effectively curtailed when he was injured bravely netting an important goal at Notts County), Cross, Brooking, Jimmy Neighbour and Paul Goddard. The latter, who had been signed the previous summer for a club record £800,000 from QPR, proved the perfect foil to 'Psycho' Cross. Goddard hit the net 17 times, while his tall partner top scored again, with 22.

West Ham achieved more than just their First Division status in 1980-81, they also enjoyed some further success in the European Cup Winners' Cup and returned to Wembley for the League Cup Final.

The Hammers' European campaign began jittery with a 3-1 defeat against Castilla in Madrid. Perceived crowd disturbances by the travelling fans led to the second leg being played behind closed doors at Upton Park. This time West Ham led 3-1 after 90 minutes to send the tie into extra-time and then scored twice more to seal the tie. Cross scored a hat-trick and was also on target when Poli Timisoara were defeated 4-0 in the first leg of the next round. A 1-0 defeat in the return game failed to derail West Ham, but Dynamo Tblisi certainly did in the quarter-final first leg. The classy Georgians played some of the most incisive football ever seen at the Boleyn Ground and ran out 4-1 winners. It was no consolation, though a major surprise, when the eventual competition winners were beaten 1-0 in the return.

In between the two clashes with Dynamo Tblisi, Lyall's side met Liverpool in the League Cup Final at Wembley. Burnley, Charlton Athletic, Barnsley, Spurs and Coventry City were knocked out en route to the final, the latter two successes against higher grade opposition. The two-legged semi-final was a real thriller. West Ham took a 2-0 half-time lead at Highfield Road through Bonds and an own-goal before the Sky Blues got their noses in front with a three goal barrage. A tense second leg was settled by second half goals from Goddard and, in the last minute, Neighbour.

A controversial goal in extra-time appeared to hand the Reds the trophy in the final, but West Ham forced a penalty in the dying moments and the reliable Stewart ensured there would be a replay. That second match was at Villa Park where a diving-header from Goddard gave the Hammers the lead and a bag full of hope. Sadly, Liverpool squeezed ahead before half-time with two soft goals and held on despite intense pressure to the great disappointment of the fervent travelling East Londoners.

There was little cup success in 1981-82, but a lot to get excited about in the League. This was particularly true at the start when West Ham's return to the top-flight was celebrated with a nine match unbeaten run, including wins at Spurs and Sunderland. Cross scored all the goals in the 4-0 rout at White Hart Lane – a triumph etched forever on every heart that has claret and blue blood running into it. However, four successive defeats in December and January hampered hopes of gaining European qualification and Lyall's side eventually finished ninth. In his last season at the club, Cross again headed the scorers' list with 16 (one more than Goddard, who won his only England cap during the following summer). The squad had been boosted by the arrival of Van der Elst and utility player Neil Orr (from Greenock Morton).

Despite two defeats in the first three games, West Ham were also among the front runners for much of the opening half of the 1982-83 campaign. Five successive wins, including a fine triumph at Highbury and a home victory over Liverpool lifted them to second place in October. However, they later struck their usual bad patch – just one win in ten games – and were sucked into the lower half of the table by the end of February. An end of term revival, when they won seven of their last ten fixtures, enabled them to finish eighth. Goddard top scored with ten goals (one more than Van der Elst) but he quite obviously missed Cross. His initial strike partner was Sandy Clark, who returned to Scotland two thirds of the way through the campaign after hitting seven goals.

Injury forced Brooking to miss all but one game of 1982-83 but he postponed his retirement by one more season and was wearing his number 10 shirt when the Hammers roared into a table-topping start to 1983-84. Opening with five wins on the trot, they reaped the benefit of a new strike-force of David Swindlehurst and a youthful Tony Cottee. With a record of just four defeats in the first 17 games, West Ham still stood proud in second place in mid-December and, despite some less consistent displays, were still in third place four months later. However, dreadful form in their last 12 games – when they won just once – meant that they drifted to ninth place. Cottee netted 15 times, two more than Swindlehurst. In the final analysis, the pivotal moment of 1983-84 probably came during the FA Cup third round tie with Wigan Athletic. The single goal victory was scant consolation for the injury that put Devonshire out for the following 19 months.

With Brooking retired (after 528 League games – 88 goals) and Devonshire recuperating, West Ham lacked creativity in 1984-85. At least Goddard had recovered from the injury that had kept him out for most of the previous season. After a promising start – which saw them in fifth spot at the end of November – the Hammers gradually faded to finish 16th, with 17 goal Cottee top scoring. Lampard (who won two England caps) waved farewell to Upton Park as a player in May 1985, having made 551 League appearances.

Most of West Ham's post-Christmas excitement in 1984-85 was provided by their best FA Cup run for five years. Port Vale (4-1) and Wimbledon (5-1) were both crushed but, in between, the Irons had to come from behind to defeat Norwich City 2-1. After three wins on their own patch, West Ham's run came to a halt at Old Trafford where Manchester United ran out 4-2 victors.

The omens did not appear good for the Hammers at the start of 1985-86 with Goddard injured in the opening day defeat at Birmingham. He failed to make another start that term and watched from the sidelines as his team-mates won only one of their first seven games to lie 17th. Yet 1985-86 turned out to be a very memorable campaign. Boosted by the return of Devonshire and two inspired signings – striker Frank McAvennie (from St. Mirren) and midfielder Mark Ward (from Oldham) – Lyall's side overcame their sluggish start to make a huge impact on the Championship race. West Ham just missed out at the death and had to settle for third place but many neutral observers agree that they consistently produced the season's best football.

McAvennie (who won four Scotland caps with West Ham) and Cottee quickly forged an excellent partnership (that eventually reaped 46 League goals that term), while a scintillating 18 match unbeaten run – including a club record nine wins on the reel – took them up to third place. However, there was a stumble in the new year when they lost a little focus due to involvement in another FA Cup run. Lyall's men reached the quarter-final with away wins over Charlton, Ipswich (in a second replay) and Manchester United (in a replay), before the disappointment was handed out by Sheffield Wednesday at Hillsborough.

The Hammers bounced back with a League win over the Owls and an unforgettable 4-0 thrashing of Chelsea at Stamford Bridge. Ironically, the rearranged return fixture with Chelsea five games later – when a fatigued side lost 2-1 – was probably the night that the title slipped away. Yet, the East Londoners responded in positive fashion with six successive wins during the nail-biting run-in. Victory at Watford was followed by an 8-1 pounding of Newcastle (with Martin netting a hat-trick against three different 'keepers'). Narrow home wins over Coventry, Manchester City and Ipswich ensured West Ham would be one of three clubs still interested in the title on the last Saturday of the season. Lyall's side carried out their task by winning 3-2 at already relegated WBA; however, the hearts of all their supporters were broken by the news filtering through from Stamford Bridge. Liverpool had beaten Chelsea to lift the title. The Hammers still had to travel to Everton for a re-arranged fixture that would decide second place. They had no stomach for it and the home side won 3-1 to leap-frog into the runner-up berth. Third place was West Ham

United's highest ever finish. Yet, it could have been so much better!

The 12 men who formed the backbone of West Ham's success in 1985-86 were Parkes, Stewart, Martin, Devonshire, Ward, McAvennie (who top scored with 26), Cottee (who netted 20 goals), Orr, Tony Gale, Alan Dickens, George Parris and Steve Walford.

Naturally there was great optimism for 1986-87, but successive home defeats early on by Nottingham Forest and Liverpool (a 5-2 shocker) suggested that the squad needed strengthening. Nevertheless, hopes were again raised when a six match unbeaten run took them up to fourth place. Yet, self-doubt set in and they won only nine of their last 32 fixtures to drift to 15th. Failure to consolidate on the success of the previous term was blamed on Lyall and the board. The cheque-book was eventually aired, but the arrival of Stewart Robson, Liam Brady, Gary Strodder and Tom McQueen came too late to make any noticeable difference. Cottee (who earned his first England caps) top scored in 1986-87 with 22 but, significantly, McAvennie netted only seven.

Matters got worse with West Ham struggling for the whole of 1987-88. They only avoided having to participate in the play-offs by defeating their main rivals Chelsea (who were subsequently relegated) 4-1 at home in the penultimate fixture and finished 16th. It was a period of great change at Upton Park. McAvennie moved to Celtic, while the injury jinxed Devonshire's campaign ended on the opening day. On a more positive note, future England international Paul Ince enjoyed his first lengthy run in the first-team and Julian Dicks arrived from Birmingham City to bolster the defence in those crucial end of season fixtures.

Cottee top scored with 13 before departing to Everton in the summer for a club record £2.2 million. Billy Bonds, who missed the whole of 1985-86 but made useful contributions in the following two campaigns, finally hung up his boots in the close season after a club record 663 League appearances (48 goals) two months short of his 42nd birthday.

Six defeats in the first eight games set the tone for an awful 1988-89 campaign. New signings David Kelly and goalie Allen McKnight were among those singled out for blame by the fans. The side failed to respond to the experience of Brady and Devonshire, and a lack of genuine fire-power proved to be a major problem. Leroy Rosenior top scored with seven (four of which were in the final four fixtures) and Kelly hit six as the Hammers mustered only 37 goals – one fewer than the number of games they played. To help boost the strike-rate McAvennie returned from Celtic for a club record £1.25 million.

A late rally of five wins in six games meant that victory at Anfield in the final fixture would have kept the Irons up. The Reds were equally desperate for the points at the other end of the table and eventually ran out 5-1 winners to plunge West Ham United into the Second Division. The difference between the sides was never as great as the scoreline suggests but that gallant display at Anfield was no consolation for the end of the club's eight term stay in the top-flight.

In contrast to their poor League form in 1988-89, West Ham embarked on lengthy runs in both cup competitions. Sunderland, Derby County, Liverpool (gloriously crushed 4-1) and Aston Villa were beaten to reach the semi-final of the Littlewoods Cup. However, two disastrous matches with Luton Town saw the Hammers crash out 5-0 on aggregate. Single goal wins accounted for Arsenal (in an away replay), Swindon Town (in a home replay) and Charlton (away) in the FA Cup, before Norwich City derailed them at Carrow Road in a sixth round replay.

Both those cup runs were little more than a distant memory when West Ham's fate in the League was sealed. Relegation (in 19th place) signalled the end of John Lyall's 15 years at the helm. At the time of his dismissal he was the Football League's longest serving manager.

Lyall's replacement was the surprise choice of Swindon boss Lou Macari. His reign came to an abrupt halt the following February, but initially his side showed promise and were comfortably placed in fifth by mid-November. A winless six match run saw them drop down to mid-table, as they embarked on another lengthy Littlewoods Cup run that took them to the semi-final stage. Top-flight Aston Villa, Wimbledon and Derby were among the scalps another Second Division side, Oldham Athletic, handed out a 6-0 St. Valentine's Day massacre in the semi-final first leg. By the time the Hammers won the meaningless second leg 3-0, a new manager and a new goalkeeper were in place. Amidst revelations of alleged financial irregularities at his old club Swindon, Macari resigned a day after his last signing, Ludek Miklosko, made his debut.

Former playing hero Billy Bonds was quickly appointed as Macari's replacement and his side won ten of the remaining 17 games to finish one place and two points short of a play-off berth in seventh place. Mid-season signing Jimmy Quinn top scored in 1989-90 with 12 goals. Long-serving Alan Devonshire (358 League games – 29 goals) and Phil Parkes (344 League games) bade farewell to the Boleyn Ground during the season. Liam Brady also signed off with a spectacular late goal in the last game (at home to Wolves) to provide a fitting end to an illustrious career.

Although five of their first eight games were drawn, West Ham quickly stamped their mark on the promotion race in 1990-91. They were not beaten in the League until their 22nd game, at Barnsley, shortly before Christmas. They then bounced back with five wins in seven games before once again becoming side-tracked by their exploits in the FA Cup. Top-flight Luton (5-0 in a replay) and Everton (2-1 in a wonderful quarter-final) were among the scalps at Upton Park as the Hammers won through to a televised Sunday semi-final meeting with Nottingham Forest at Villa Park. Bonds' side were more than holding their own against Brian Clough's First Division outfit until referee Keith Hackett harshly dismissed Tony Gale. Forest made hay to the tune of four goals, but despite this the West Ham faithful chanted themselves hoarse in a magnificent show of defiance in adversity.

Promotion was never in doubt and although key points were squandered in the run-in, West Ham reached the final game of the season – at home to Notts County – knowing that victory would give them the title. However, a lacklustre display and a 2-1 defeat gave Oldham the chance to snatch the Crown – and they did so, courtesy of a late spot-kick victory at Boundary Park. The Hammers had to be content with second place.

The key players in West Ham's 1990-91 promotion winning squad were: Steve Potts, Colin Foster, Kevin Keen, Ian Bishop, Stuart Slater, Martin Allen, Trevor Morley (who top scored with 12 goals), Tim Breacker, Chris Hughton, Parris, Gale, McAvennie and the ever-present Miklosko. In addition, Dicks and Martin made useful contributions early in the term before succumbing to injury. Penalty king Ray Stewart (who won ten Scotland caps with West Ham) made his 345th and last League appearance (62 goals) in 1990-91.

The Irons made a shaky return to the top-flight, winning just two of the first 13 fixtures. Consecutive victories over Spurs and Arsenal (at Highbury) provided hope of an upturn in fortunes. Sadly, though, only five more League games were won as the Hammers crashed back to the second-flight in 22nd and bottom position. Two of those wins came in the last three games – Manchester United's title hopes being torpedoed by a Kenny Brown special and Nottingham Forest falling foul of McAvennie who came off the bench to net a hat-trick in his farewell game. Failure to take chances was their achilles heel in that extremely disappointing 1991-92 campaign. In total the Hammers netted just 37 times – the top scorer was Mike Small but only three of his 13 came in the final 27 games.

In contrast, West Ham could not stop scoring in 1992-93 and earned automatic promotion by netting 81 times to finish second behind Kevin Keegan's formidable Newcastle outfit. Bonds' side never looked like catching the long-term leaders and, in fact, had their work cut out to hold off the threat from Jim Smith's Portsmouth (whose hopes of elevation were ultimately to be snuffed out in the play-offs) for the only other automatic promotion berth. West Ham eventually secured the runners-up spot with a fourth successive victory (over Cambridge United at home) on the final day of the season. However, the key result came six days earlier when they defeated Swindon 3-1 at the County Ground.

Morley top scored (with 20 goals), while the other main-stays in 1992-93 were Miklosko, Potts, Breacker, Dicks, Martin (until injury again curtailed his campaign at the halfway stage), Gale, Keen, Martin Allen, Clive Allen, Mark Robson and Peter Butler. Another vital contribution came from on-loan David Speedie who bolstered the attack during the tension-packed last 11 fixtures.

During their promotion campaign, West Ham United was rocked by the shock news of the death of Bobby Moore, on 24th February 1993. The finest footballer that the club had produced had succumbed to cancer.

West Ham struggled during the early stages of their first taste of Premiership football, winning just one of their first seven games. Meanwhile the popular Dicks was transferred to Liverpool. However, new signings Lee Chapman, David Burrows and Mike Marsh bedded in quickly and the Hammers climbed to mid-table by the turn of the year. A nine match winless run threatened to destroy all their earlier good work, but four victories in the final nine games ensured they finished 1993-94 in a respectable 13th place. Morley top scored for the third season in four (with 13 goals) and Tony Gale made his 300th and last League appearance for West Ham.

The Boleyn Ground faithful had high hopes of a successful FA Cup run in 1994, with Watford, Notts County and Kidderminster Harriers being side-stepped before second-flight Luton derailed West Ham in a sixth round replay.

East London was rocked by a huge bombshell ten days before the start of 1994-95 when Billy Bonds resigned and was replaced by his assistant Harry Redknapp. On the pitch, the Hammers always struggled after a poor start in which they failed to win any of their first five fixtures. The return of former favourites Tony Cottee and Julian Dicks lifted the morale, but only once – in early October – were victories secured in two successive League games. However, by avoiding defeat in all but two of the last 13 fixtures, Redknapp's side pulled clear of relegation by five points in 14th place. Cottee was the main marksman, with 13 goals.

Twelve months later Cottee was joint top scorer with Dicks, on the ten goal mark. West Ham overcame another sluggish start (two points from the first six games) to gradually climb to mid-table respectability. Redknapp's side eventually finished tenth after five successive wins in mid-winter burnt away the fears of being sucked back into relegation trouble. There was no cup joy in 1995-96 with First Division Grimsby Town knocking them out of the FA Cup in a fourth round replay. Veteran centre-half Alvin Martin left Upton Park at the end of the campaign, after making 469 League appearances.

Yet another poor start meant West Ham spent the whole of 1996-97 battling against relegation. Redknapp had packed his squad with a clutch of experienced foreign internationals. The disappointing Florin Raducioiu, Ilie Dumitrescu and the crocked Paulo Futre failed to last out; but more meaningful contributions did come from other overseas stars such as the long serving Miklosko, Marc Rieper, Slaven

Bilic and on-loan striker Hugo Porfirio. Even so, West Ham were knocked out of both cup competitions by Second Division sides (Stockport County and Wrexham) and in mid-February still looked very good bets for relegation. The pivotal moment of the campaign was not on the pitch, but behind the scenes when Redknapp was given the green light to hire some new guns. Strikers Paul Kitson (top scorer with 8 goals) and £3.2 million club record buy John Hartson (5 goals) gelled immediately, while another late season purchase Steve Lomas added extra grit to the midfield. With only two defeats in the last 11 games, the Irons edged clear of danger by two points in 14th place.

West Ham's fifth Premiership campaign was to be their most successful and in addition they enjoyed lengthy runs in the two cup competitions. Upton Park victories over Huddersfield Town, Aston Villa and Walsall took the Hammers into the Coca-Cola Cup quarter-final. However, a visit by Arsenal halted their progress. It was the Gunners who also ended West Ham's dreams of FA Cup glory in a quarter-final replay. The North Londoners – who ultimately ended the season as 'Double' winners – triumphed in a penalty shoot-out after playing all but the first 30 minutes with 10 men. The Hammers had succeeded in a shoot-out themselves in a replay at Blackburn in the previous round, after earlier knocking out Emley (at home) and Manchester City (away).

In the League, a solid start of three victories in five games appeared to be wasted by a run of seven defeats in nine fixtures. However, Redknapp's side proved almost impregnable at home, winning nine out of their first ten Upton Park fixtures to move back into the top half of the table. Losing just two home League games all term, Redknapp's men finished eighth but just missed out on UEFA Cup qualification by one place and one point. They slipped up by conceding 15 goals and dropping eight points during the last four games of the season. It was still a memorable campaign, though, with the first West Ham player – Rio Ferdinand – to be capped for England in over nine years. The 19 year-old, who impressed enough to secure a place in Glenn Hoddle's World Cup squad, was one of several Hammers to make sizable contributions in 1997-98. Hartson top scored (with 15), while Lomas (appointed Northern Ireland skipper), Stan Lazaridis and Frank Lampard Junior added to their growing reputations. With the acquisitions of Eyal Berkovic, Ian Pearce and Trevor Sinclair, the West Ham United squad was bulging with more quality than at any stage in the previous 25 years.

F.A. CUP

1973-74 SEASON
3rd Round
Jan 5 vs Hereford United (h) 1-1
Att: 23,087   Holland

Replay
Jan 9 vs Hereford United (a) 1-2
Att: 17,423   Best

1974-75 SEASON
3rd Round
Jan 4 vs Southampton (a) 2-1
Att: 24,615   Lampard, Gould

4th Round
Jan 25 vs Swindon Town (h) 1-1
Att: 35,679   Jennings

Replay
Jan 28 vs Swindon Town (a) 2-1
Att: 26,749   Brooking, Holland

5th Round
Feb 15 vs Queen's Park Rangers (h) 2-1
Att: 39,193   Holland, Robson

6th Round
Mar 8 vs Arsenal (a) 2-0
Att: 56,742   Taylor A 2

Semi-Final (at Villa Park)
Apr 5 vs Ipswich Town   0-0
Att: 58,000

Replay (at Stamford Bridge)
Apr 9 vs Ipswich Town   2-1
Att: 45,344   Taylor A 2

FINAL (at Wembley)
May 3 vs Fulham   2-0
Att: 100,000   Taylor A 2

1975-76 SEASON
3rd Round
Jan 3 vs Liverpool (h) 0-2
Att: 32,363

1976-77 SEASON
3rd Round
Jan 8 vs Bolton Wanderers (h) 2-1
Att: 24,147   Jennings, Pike

4th Round
Jan 29 vs Aston Villa (a) 0-3
Att: 46,954

1977-78 SEASON
3rd Round
Jan 7 vs Watford (h) 1-0
Att: 36,475   Robson

4th Round
Jan 28 vs Queen's Park Rangers (h) 1-1
Att: 35,556   Bonds

Replay
Jan 31 vs Queen's Park Rangers (a) 1-6
Att: 24,057   Robson

1978-79 SEASON
3rd Round
Jan 9 vs Newport County (a) 1-2
Att: 14,124   Robson

1979-80 SEASON
3rd Round
Jan 5 vs West Bromwich Albion (h) 1-1
Att: 20,572   Pearson

Replay
Jan 8 vs West Bromwich Albion (h) 2-1
Att: 30,689   Pike, Brooking

4th Round
Jan 26 vs Orient (a) 3-2
Att: 21,521   Gray (og), Stewart 2 (1 pen)

5th Round
Feb 16 vs Swansea City (h) 2-0
Att: 30,497   Allen, Cross

6th Round
Mar 8 vs Aston Villa (h) 1-0
Att: 36,393   Stewart (pen)

Semi-Final (at Villa Park)
Apr 12 vs Everton   1-1
Att: 47,685   Pearson

Replay (at Elland Road)
Apr 16 vs Everton   2-1 (aet) (90 mins. 0-0)
Att: 40,720   Devonshire, Lampard

FINAL (at Wembley)
May 10 vs Arsenal   1-0
Att: 100,000   Brooking

1980-81 SEASON
3rd Round
Jan 3 vs Wrexham (h) 1-1
Att: 30,137   Stewart (pen)

Replay
Jan 6 vs Wrexham (a) 0-0 (aet)
Att: 13,643

2nd Replay
Jan 19 vs Wrexham (a) 0-1 (aet)
Att: 14,615

1981-82 SEASON
3rd Round
Jan 2 vs Everton (h) 2-1
Att: 24,431   Bonds, Cross

4th Round
Jan 23 vs Watford (a) 0-2
Att: 27,004

1982-83 SEASON
3rd Round
Jan 8 vs Manchester United (a) 0-2
Att: 44,143

1983-84 SEASON
3rd Round
Jan 7 vs Wigan Athletic (h) 1-0
Att: 16,000   Stewart (pen)

4th Round
Jan 28 vs Crystal Palace (a) 1-1
Att: 27,590   Swindlehurst

Replay
Jan 31 vs Crystal Palace (h) 2-0
Att: 27,127   Pike, Barnes

5th Round
Feb 18 vs Birmingham City (a) 0-3
Att: 29,570

1984-85 SEASON
3rd Round
Jan 5 vs Port Vale (h) 4-1
Att: 11,452   Dickens, Goddard 3

4th Round
Feb 4 vs Norwich City (h) 2-1
Att: 20,098   Pike, Stewart (pen)

5th Round
Mar 4 vs Wimbledon (h) 1-1
Att: 13,500   Cottee

Replay
Mar 6 vs Wimbledon (h) 5-1
Att: 20,258   Cottee 3, Dickens, Allen

6th Round
Mar 9 vs Manchester United (a) 2-4
Att: 46,769   Hogg (og), Allen

1985-86 SEASON
3rd Round
Jan 5 vs Charlton Athletic (a) 1-0
Att: 13,037   Cottee

4th Round
Jan 25 vs Ipswich Town (h) 0-0
Att: 25,035

Replay
Feb 4 vs Ipswich Town (a) 1-1 (aet) (90 minutes 0-0)
Att: 25,384   Cottee

2nd Replay
Feb 6 vs Ipswich Town (a) 1-0 (aet)
Att: 14,515   Cottee

5th Round
Mar 5 vs Manchester United (h) 1-1
Att: 26,441   McAvennie

Replay
Mar 9 vs Manchester United (a) 2-0
Att: 30,441   Pike, Stewart (pen)

6th Round
Mar 12 vs Sheffield Wednesday (a) 1-2
Att: 35,522   Cottee

1986-87 SEASON
3rd Round
Jan 10 vs Orient (a) 1-1
Att: 19,225   Hilton

Replay
Jan 31 vs Orient (h) 4-1
Att: 19,424   Parris, Keen, McAvennie, Cottee

4th Round
Feb 9 vs Sheffield United (h) 4-0
Att: 17,194   McAvennie 2, Robson, Gale

5th Round
Feb 21 vs Sheffield Wednesday (a) 1-1
Att: 31,134   McAvennie

Replay
Feb 25 vs Sheffield Wednesday (h) 0-2
Att: 30,257

1987-88 SEASON
3rd Round
Jan 9 vs Charlton Athletic (h) 2-0
Att: 22,043   Brady, Cottee

4th Round
Jan 30 vs Queen's Park Rangers (a) 1-3
Att: 23,651   Cottee

1988-89 SEASON
3rd Round
Jan 8 vs Arsenal (h) 2-2
Att: 22,017   Dickens, Bould (og)

Replay
Jan 11 vs Arsenal (a) 1-0
Att: 44,124   Rosenior

4th Round
Jan 28 vs Swindon Town (a) 0-0
Att: 18,627

Replay
Feb 1 vs Swindon Town (h) 1-0
Att: 24,723   Rosenior

5th Round
Feb 18 vs Charlton Athletic (a) 1-0
Att: 18,785   Slater

6th Round
Mar 18 vs Norwich City (h) 0-0
Att: 29,119

14

Replay
Mar 22 vs Norwich City (a) 1-3
Att: 25,785 Ince

1989-90 SEASON
3rd Round
Jan 6 vs Torquay United (a) 0-1
Att: 5,342

1990-91 SEASON
3rd Round
Jan 5 vs Aldershot (a) 0-0
Att: 22,929
Replay
Jan 16 vs Aldershot (h) 6-1
*Att: 21,484 Morley 2, Slater, Parris,
Bishop, Quinn*
4th Round
Jan 26 vs Luton Town (a) 1-1
Att: 12,087 Parris
Replay
Jan 30 vs Luton Town (h) 5-0
*Att: 25,659 Parris, Bishop, McAvennie,
Morley 2*
5th Round
Feb 16 vs Crewe Alexandra (h) 1-0
Att: 25,298 Quinn
6th Round
Mar 11 vs Everton (h) 2-1
Att: 28,161 Foster, Slater
Semi-Final (at Villa Park)
Apr 14 vs Nottingham Forest 0-4
Att: 40,041

1991-92 SEASON
3rd Round (at Upton Park)
Jan 4 vs Farnborough Town (a) 1-1
Att: 23,449 Dicks
Replay
Jan 14 vs Farnborough Town (h) 1-0
Att: 23,869 Morley
4th Round
Jan 25 vs Wrexham (h) 2-2
Att: 24,712 Dicks, Morley
Replay
Feb 4 vs Wrexham (a) 1-0
Att: 17,995 Foster
5th Round
Feb 15 vs Sunderland (a) 1-1
Att: 25,475 Small
Replay
Feb 26 vs Sunderland (h) 2-3
Att: 25,830 Allen 2

1992-93 SEASON
3rd Round
Jan 2 vs West Bromwich Albion (a) 2-0
Att: 25,896 Allen C, Robson
4th Round
Jan 24 vs Barnsley (a) 1-4
Att: 13,716 Morley (pen)

1993-94 SEASON
3rd Round
Jan 8 vs Watford (h) 2-1
Att: 19,802 Allen M, Marsh
4th Round
Jan 29 vs Notts County (a) 1-1
Att: 14,952 Jones
Replay
Feb 9 vs Notts County (h) 1-0 (aet)
Att: 23,373 Chapman

5th Round
Feb 19 vs Kidderminster Harriers (a) 1-0
Att: 8,000 Chapman
6th Round
Mar 14 vs Luton Town (h) 0-0
Att: 27,331
Replay
Mar 23 vs Luton Town (a) 2-3
Att: 13,166 Allen M, Bishop

1994-95 SEASON
3rd Round
Jan 7 vs Wycombe Wanderers (a) 2-0
Att: 9,007 Cottee, Brown
4th Round
Jan 28 vs Queen's Park Rangers (h) 0-1
Att: 17,694

1995-96 SEASON
3rd Round
Jan 6 vs Southend United (h) 2-0
Att: 11,059 Moncur, Hughes
4th Round
Feb 7 vs Grimsby Town (h) 1-1
Att: 22,030 Dowie
Replay
Feb 14 vs Grimsby Town (a) 0-3
Att: 8,382

1996-97 SEASON
3rd Round
Jan 4 vs Wrexham (a) 1-1
Att: 9,747 Porfirio
Replay
Jan 25 vs Wrexham (h) 0-1
Att: 16,763

1997-98 SEASON
3rd Round
Jan 3 vs Emley (h) 2-1
Att: 18,629 Lampard, Hartson
4th Round
Jan 25 vs Manchester City (a) 2-1
Att: 26,495 Berkovic, Lomas
5th Round
Feb 14 vs Blackburn Rovers (h) 2-2
Att: 25,729 Kitson, Berkovic
Replay
Feb 25 vs Blackburn Rovers (a) 1-1 (aet)
Att: 21,972 Hartson
West Ham United won 5-4 on penalties
6th Round
Mar 8 vs Arsenal (a) 1-1
Att: 38,077 Pearce
Replay
Mar 17 vs Arsenal (h) 1-1 (aet)
Att: 25,859 Hartson
Arsenal won 4-3 on penalties

LEAGUE CUP
1973-74 SEASON
2nd Round
Oct 8 vs Liverpool (h) 2-2
Att: 25,840 McDougall, Robson
Replay
Oct 29 vs Liverpool (a) 0-1
Att: 26,002

1974-75 SEASON
2nd Round
Sep 11 vs Tranmere Rovers (a) 0-0
Att: 8,638

Replay
Sep 18 vs Tranmere Rovers (h) 6-0
Att: 15,854 Bonds 2 (1 pen), Gould 3, Ayris
3rd Round
Oct 8 vs Fulham (a) 1-2
Att: 29,611 Brooking

1975-76 SEASON
2nd Round
Sep 9 vs Bristol City (h) 0-0
Att: 19,837
Replay
Sep 24 vs Bristol City (a) 3-1
Att: 19,634 Brooking, Best, Taylor A
3rd Round
Oct 7 vs Darlington (h) 3-0
Att: 19,844 Paddon, Bonds (pen), Robson
4th Round
Nov 11 vs Tottenham Hotspur (a) 0-0
Att: 49,125
Replay
Nov 24 vs Tottenham Hotspur (h) 0-2 (aet)
Att: 38,443

1976-77 SEASON
2nd Round
Sep 1 vs Barnsley (h) 3-0
Att: 17,889 Holland 2, Paddon
3rd Round
Sep 21 vs Charlton Athletic (a) 1-0
Att: 34,000 Taylor A
4th Round
Oct 27 vs Queen's Park Rangers (h) 0-2
Att: 24,565

1977-78 SEASON
2nd Round
Aug 30 vs Nottingham Forest (a) 0-5
Att: 18,224

1978-79 SEASON
2nd Round
Aug 30 vs Swindon Town (h) 1-2
Att: 19,672 Robson

1979-80 SEASON
2nd Round (1st leg)
Aug 28 vs Barnsley (h) 3-1
Att: 12,320 Brooking, Pearson, Cross
2nd Round (2nd leg)
Sep 4 vs Barnsley (a) 2-0 (aggregate 5-1)
Att: 15,898 Cross 2
3rd Round
Sep 25 vs Southend (h) 1-1
Att: 19,658 Cross
Replay
Oct 1 vs Southend (a) 0-0 (aet)
Att: 22,497
2nd Replay
Oct 8 vs Southend 5-1
*Att: 19,718 Lansdowne 3, Holland,
Stewart (pen)*
4th Round
Oct 31 vs Sunderland (a) 1-1
Att: 30,302 Pike
Replay
Nov 5 vs Sunderland (h) 2-1
Att: 24,454 Martin, Cross
5th Round
Dec 4 vs Nottingham Forest (h) 0-0
Att: 35,856

15

Replay
Dec 12 vs Nottingham Forest (a) 0-3 (aet)
Att: 25,462

1980-81 SEASON
2nd Round (1st leg)
Aug 26 vs Burnley (a) 2-0
Att: 6,818   Goddard, Cross

2nd Round (2nd leg)
Sep 2 vs Burnley (h) 4-0   (aggregate 6-0)
Att: 15,216   Stewart (pen), Goddard,
Wood (og), Pike

3rd Round
Sep 23 vs Charlton Athletic (a) 2-1
Att: 17,884   Cross 2

4th Round
Oct 28 vs Barnsley (h) 2-1
Att: 21,548   Martin, Cross

5th Round
Dec 2 vs Tottenham Hotspur (h) 1-0
Att: 36,003   Cross

Semi-Final (1st leg)
Jan 27 vs Coventry City (a) 2-3
Att: 35,468   Bonds, Thompson (og)

Semi-Final (2nd leg)
Feb 10 vs Coventry City (h) 2-0 (agg. 4-3)
Att: 36,551   Goddard, Neighbour

FINAL (at Wembley)
Mar 14 vs Liverpool 1-1 (aet) (90 mins. 0-0)
Att: 100,000   Stewart (pen)

Replay (at Villa Park)
Apr 1 vs Liverpool   1-2
Att: 36,693   Goddard

1981-82 SEASON
2nd Round (1st leg)
Oct 7 vs Derby County (a) 3-2
Att: 13,764   Cross, Brooking, Stewart (pen)

2nd Round (2nd leg)
Oct 27 vs Derby County (h) 2-0 (agg. 5-2)
Att: 21,043   Goddard 2

3rd Round
Nov 10 vs West Bromwich Albion (h) 2-2
Att: 24,168   Stewart (pen), Cross

Replay
Nov 24 vs West Bromwich Albion (a) 1-1
(aet) (90 minutes 0-0)
Att: 15,869   Stewart (pen)

2nd Replay
Dec 1 vs West Bromwich Albion (h) 0-1
Att: 24,760

1982-83 SEASON
2nd Round (1st leg)
Oct 6 vs Stoke City (a) 1-1
Att: 18,079   Stewart (pen)

2nd Round (2nd leg)
Oct 26 vs Stoke City (h) 2-1 (aggregate 3-2)
Att: 18,270   Goddard, Clark

3rd Round
Nov 10 vs Lincoln City (a) 1-1
Att: 13,899   Goddard

Replay
Nov 29 vs Lincoln City (h) 2-1 (aet) (90
minutes 1-1)
Att: 13,686   Stewart, Clark

4th Round
Dec 7 vs Notts County (a) 3-3
Att: 7,525   Van der Elst 3

Replay
Dec 21 vs Notts County (h) 3-0
Att: 13,140   Stewart (pen), Clark, Allen

5th Round
Jan 18 vs Liverpool (a) 1-2
Att: 23,953   Allen

1983-84 SEASON
2nd Round (1st leg)
Oct 4 vs Bury (a) 2-1
Att: 8,050   Goddard, Orr

2nd Round (2nd leg)
Oct 25 vs Bury (h) 10-0   (aggregate 12-1)
Att: 10,896   Cottee 4, Martin, Stewart (pen),
Brooking 2, Devonshire 2

3rd Round
Nov 8 vs Brighton & Hove Albion (h) 1-0
Att: 17,082   Swindlehurst

4th Round
Nov 30 vs Everton (h) 2-2
Att: 19,702   Mountfield (og), Pike

Replay
Dec 6 vs Everton (a) 0-2 (aet)
Att: 21,609

1984-85 SEASON
2nd Round (1st leg)
Sep 25 vs Bristol City (a) 2-2
Att: 15,894   Cottee, Walford

2nd Round (2nd leg)
Oct 9 vs Bristol City (h) 6-1 (aggregate 8-3)
Att: 11,376   Cottee 2, Goddard 2, Whitton,
Walford

3rd Round
Oct 31 vs Manchester City (a) 0-0
Att: 20,510

Replay
Nov 6 vs Manchester City (h) 1-2
Att: 17,461   Whitton

1985-86 SEASON
2nd Round (1st leg)
Sep 24 vs Swansea City (h) 3-0
Att: 9,282   Cottee, McAvennie, Stewart (pen)

2nd Round (2nd leg)
Oct 8 vs Swansea City (a) 3-2 (agg. 6-2)
Att: 3,584   Stewart 2 (2 pens), Cottee

3rd Round
Oct 29 vs Manchester United (a) 0-1
Att: 32,057

1986-87 SEASON
2nd Round (1st leg)
Sep 23 vs Preston North End (a) 1-1
Att: 13,153   Ward

2nd Round (2nd leg)
Oct 7 vs Preston N. End (h) 4-1 (agg. 5-2)
Att: 12,742   Cottee 3, Dickens

3rd Round
Oct 29 vs Watford (a) 3-2
Att: 17,523   Goddard, Dickens, Ward

4th Round
Nov 18 vs Oxford United (h) 1-0
Att: 20,530   Cottee (pen)

5th Round
Jan 27 vs Tottenham Hotspur (h) 1-1
Att: 29,477   Cottee

Replay
Feb 2 vs Tottenham Hotspur (a) 0-5
Att: 41,995

1987-88 SEASON
2nd Round (1st leg)
Sep 22 vs Barnsley (a) 0-0
Att: 10,330

2nd Round (2nd leg)
Oct 6 vs Barnsley (h) 2-5 (aet)(90 mins. 2-2)
Att: 12,403   Keen, Robson

1988-89 SEASON
2nd Round (1st leg)
Sep 27 vs Sunderland (a) 3-0
Att: 13,691   Kelly 2, Rosenior

2nd Round (2nd leg)
Oct 12 vs Sunderland (h) 2-1 (agg. 5-1)
Att: 10,558   Kelly, Dickens

3rd Round
Nov 1 vs Derby County (h) 5-0
Att: 14,226   Martin 2, Stewart (pen),
Rosenior, Keen

4th Round
Nov 30 vs Liverpool (h) 4-1
Att: 26,971   Ince 2, Staunton (og), Gale

5th Round
Jan 18 vs Aston Villa (h) 2-1
Att: 30,110   Ince, Kelly

Semi-Final (1st leg)
Feb 12 vs Luton Town (h) 0-3
Att: 24,602

Semi-Final (2nd leg)
Mar 1 vs Luton Town (a) 0-2 (agg. 0-5)
Att: 12,020

1989-90 SEASON
2nd Round (1st leg)
Sep 19 vs Birmingham City (a) 2-1
Att: 10,987   Allen, Slater

2nd Round (2nd leg)
Oct 4 vs Birmingham City (h) 1-1 (agg. 3-2)
Att: 12,187   Dicks

3rd Round
Oct 25 vs Aston Villa (a) 0-0
Att: 20,989

Replay
Nov 8 vs Aston Villa (h) 1-0
Att: 23,833   Dicks

4th Round
Nov 22 vs Wimbledon (h) 1-0
Att: 24,746   Allen

5th Round
Jan 17 vs Derby County (h) 1-1
Att: 25,035   Dicks

Replay
Jan 24 vs Derby County (a) 0-0 (aet)
Att: 22,510

2nd Replay
Jan 31 vs Derby County (h) 2-1
Att: 25,166   Slater, Keen

Semi-Final (1st leg)
Feb 14 vs Oldham Athletic (a) 0-6
Att: 19,263

Semi-Final (2nd leg)
Mar 7 vs Oldham Athletic (h) 3-0 (agg. 3-6)
Att: 15,431   Martin, Dicks (pen), Kelly

1990-91 SEASON
2nd Round (1st leg)
Sep 26 vs Stoke City (h) 3-0
Att: 15,870   Dicks (pen), Keen, Quinn

2nd Round (2nd leg)
Oct 10 vs Stoke City (a) 2-1 (agg. 5-1)
Att: 8,411   Allen 2

16

3rd Round
Oct 31 vs Oxford United (a) 1-2
Att: 7,528   Morley

1991-92 SEASON
2nd Round (1st leg)
Sep 24 vs Bradford City (a) 1-1
Att: 7,034   Small

2nd Round (2nd leg)
Oct 9 vs Bradford City (h) 4-0 (agg. 5-1)
Att: 17,232   Keen, Morley, Parris, Small

3rd Round
Oct 29 vs Sheffield United (a) 2-0
Att: 11,144   McAvennie, Small (pen)

4th Round
Dec 4 vs Norwich City (a) 1-2
Att: 16,325   Small

1992-93 SEASON
2nd Round (1st leg)
Sep 23 vs Crewe Alexandra (h) 0-0
Att: 6,981

2nd Round (2nd leg)
Oct 7 vs Crewe Alexandra (a) 0-2 (agg. 0-2)
Att: 5,427

1993-94 SEASON
2nd Round (1st leg)
Sep 22 vs Chesterfield (h) 5-1
Att: 12,823   Morley 2 (1 pen), Chapman 2, Burrows

2nd Round (2nd leg)
Oct 5 vs Chesterfield (a) 2-0 (agg. 7-1)
Att: 4,890   Allen M, Boere

3rd Round
Oct 27 vs Nottingham Forest (a) 1-2
Att: 17,857   Morley

1994-95 SEASON
2nd Round (1st leg)
Sep 20 vs Walsall (a) 1-2
Att: 5,994   Ntamark (og)

2nd Round (2nd leg)
Oct 5 vs Walsall (h) 2-0 (aet) (90 mins. 1-0)
Att: 13,553   Hutchison, Moncur

3rd Round
Oct 26 vs Chelsea (h) 1-0
Att: 18,815   Hutchison

4th Round
Nov 30 vs Bolton Wanderers (h) 1-3
Att: 18,190   Cottee

1995-96 SEASON
2nd Round (1st leg)
Sep 20 vs Bristol Rovers (a) 1-0
Att: 7,103   Moncur

2nd Round (2nd leg)
Oct 4 vs Bristol Rovers (h) 3-0 (agg. 4-0)
Att: 15,375   Dicks (pen), Bishop, Cottee

3rd Round
Oct 25 vs Southampton (a) 1-2
Att: 11,059   Cottee

1996-97 SEASON
2nd Round (1st leg)
Sep 18 vs Barnet (a) 1-1
Att: 3,849   Cottee

2nd Round (2nd leg)
Sep 25 vs Barnet (h) 1-0 (aggregate 2-1)
Att: 15,264   Bilic

3rd Round
Oct 23 vs Nottingham Forest (h) 4-1
Att: 19,402   Dowie 2, Porfirio, Dicks

4th Round
Nov 27 vs Stockport County (h) 1-1
Att: 20,061   Raducioiu

Replay
Dec 18 vs Stockport County (a) 1-2
Att: 9,834   Dicks

1997-98 SEASON
2nd Round (1st leg)
Sep 16 vs Huddersfield Town (h) 0-1
Att: 8,525

2nd Round (2nd leg)
Sep 29 vs Huddersfield T. (a) 3-0 (agg. 3-1)
Att: 16,137   Hartson 3

3rd Round
Oct 15 vs Aston Villa (h) 3-0
Att: 20,360   Hartson 2, Lampard

4th Round
Nov 19 vs Walsall (h) 4-1
Att: 17,463   Lampard 3, Hartson

5th Round
Jan 6 vs Arsenal (h) 1-2
Att: 24,770   Abou

EUROPEAN CUP-WINNERS-CUP

1975-76 SEASON
1st Round (1st leg)
Sep 17 vs Lahden Reipas (a) 2-2
Att: 4,587   Brooking, Bonds

1st Round (2nd leg)
Oct 1 vs Lahden Reipas (h) 3-0 (agg. 5-2)
Att: 24,131   Robson, Holland, Jennings

2nd Round (1st leg)
Oct 22 vs Ararat Erevan (a) 1-1
Att: 66,662   Taylor A

2nd Round (2nd leg)
Nov 5 vs Ararat Erevan (h) 3-1 (agg. 4-2)
Att: 30,399   Paddon, Robson, Taylor A

Quarter-Final (1st leg)
Mar 3 vs Den Haag (a) 2-4
Att: 26,000   Jennings 2

Quarter-Final (2nd leg)
Mar 17 vs Den Haag (h) 3-1 (agg. 5-5)
Att: 29,829   Taylor A, Lampard, Bonds
West Ham won on the Away Goals rule

Semi-Final (1st leg)
Mar 31 vs Eintracht Frankfurt (a) 1-2
Att: 45,000   Paddon

Semi-Final (2nd leg)
Apr 14 vs Eintr. Frankfurt (h) 3-1 (agg. 4-3)
Att: 39,202   Brooking 2, Robson

FINAL (at Heysel Stadium)
May 5 vs Anderlecht 2-4
Att: 58,000   Holland, Robson

1980-81 SEASON
1st Round (1st leg)
Sep 17 vs Castilla (a) 1-3
Att: 40,000   Cross

1st Round (2nd leg)
Oct 1 vs Castilla (h) 5-1 (aet) (agg 6-4) (90 minutes 3-1)
Played behind closed doors
Scorers: Pike, Cross 3, Goddard

2nd Round (1st leg)
Oct 22 vs Politecnica Timisoara (h) 4-0
Att: 27,257   Bonds, Goddard, Stewart (pen), Cross

2nd Round (2nd leg)
Nov 5 vs Poli. Timisoara (a) 0-1 (agg. 4-1)
Att: 25,000

3rd Round (1st leg)
Mar 4 vs Dynamo Tbilisi (h) 1-4
Att: 34,957   Cross

3rd Round (2nd leg)
Mar 18 vs Dynamo Tbilisi (a) 1-0 (agg. 2-4)
Att: 80,000   Pearson

1973-74

1	Aug	25	(h)	Newcastle U	L	1-2	Robson	28,169
2		27	(h)	Ipswich T	D	3-3	Best, Bonds, Brooking	23,335
3	Sep	1	(a)	Norwich C	D	2-2	Best, Robson	25,706
4		4	(a)	Queen's Park R	D	0-0		28,360
5		8	(h)	Tottenham H	L	0-1		30,888
6		10	(h)	Queen's Park R	L	2-3	Robson, Bonds (pen)	26,042
7		15	(a)	Manchester U	L	1-3	Bonds (pen)	44,757
8		22	(h)	Leicester C	D	1-1	Robson	23,567
9		29	(a)	Stoke C	L	0-2		16,395
10	Oct	6	(h)	Burnley	L	0-1		23,604
11		13	(a)	Everton	L	0-1		34,608
12		20	(a)	Coventry C	W	1-0	McDowell	21,097
13		27	(h)	Derby Co	D	0-0		31,237
14	Nov	3	(a)	Leeds U	L	1-4	MacDougall	36,869
15		10	(h)	Sheffield U	D	2-2	Bonds, Brooking	21,243
16		17	(a)	Wolverhampton W	D	0-0		19,587
17		24	(h)	Arsenal	L	1-3	Bonds	28,287
18	Dec	1	(a)	Liverpool	L	0-1		34,857
19		8	(h)	Manchester C	W	2-1	Brooking, Doyle (og)	20,790
20		15	(a)	Birmingham C	L	1-3	Gould	23,767
21		22	(h)	Stoke C	L	0-2		16,513
22		26	(a)	Chelsea	W	4-2	Best 2, Gould, Lampard	26,982
23		29	(a)	Tottenham H	L	0-2		33,172
24	Jan	1	(h)	Norwich C	W	4-2	Paddon 2, Brooking, Gould	32,259
25		12	(h)	Manchester U	W	2-1	Bonds, Holland	34,147
26		19	(a)	Newcastle U	D	1-1	Holland	27,404
27	Feb	2	(h)	Birmingham C	D	0-0		27,948
28		5	(a)	Ipswich T	W	3-1	Mills (og), McDowell, Best	25,747
29		9	(a)	Leicester C	W	1-0	Best	27,032
30		16	(h)	Everton	W	4-3	Best 2, Bonds, Paddon	29,347
31		23	(a)	Burnley	D	1-1	Paddon	18,216
32	Mar	2	(h)	Chelsea	W	3-0	Bonds 3	34,043
33		9	(a)	Derby Co	D	1-1	Bond	24,684
34		16	(h)	Coventry C	L	2-3	Bonds 2 (1 pen)	26,502
35		23	(a)	Sheffield U	L	0-1		19,467
36		30	(h)	Leeds U	W	3-1	Best, Brooking, Robson	37,480
37	Apr	6	(a)	Arsenal	D	0-0		37,868
38		12	(h)	Southampton	W	4-1	Best 2, Robson 2	34,163
39		13	(h)	Wolverhampton W	D	0-0		29,488
40		15	(a)	Southampton	D	1-1	Best	26,515
41		20	(a)	Manchester C	L	1-2	Gould	29,700
42		27	(h)	Liverpool	D	2-2	Brooking, Lampard	36,160

FINAL LEAGUE POSITION: 18th in Division One

Appearances

Sub. Appearances

Goals

Ferguson	Lampard	Charles	Bonds	Taylor	Moore	Best	Lutton	MacDougall	Brooking	Robson	Holland	Day	Lock	Ayris	McDowell	Tyler	Coker	Coleman	Gould	McGiven	Paddon	Wooler	
1	2	3	4	5	6	7*	8	9	10	11	12												1
	2		4	5	6	7		9	10	11	8	1	3										2
1	2		4	5	6	7	8		10	11	9		3										3
1	2		4	5	6	7			10	11	8		3	9									4
1	3		4	5	6	7		9*	10	11	12		8		2								5
1	3		4	5	6			9	10	11	8				2	7							6
1	3		4	5		12		9	10	11	8		6		2	7*							7
1	3		4	5	6			9*	10	11	8				2	7	12						8
1	3		4	5	6			9	10	11	8				2	7							9
	3		4		6	7*		9	10	11	8	1	12	5	2								10
	3		4	5	6	8		9	10	11		1	7		2								11
	3		4	5	6			9	10	11*		1	12		8	7		2					12
	3		4	5	6			9	10			1	11		8	7		2					13
	3		4	5	6			9	11	10		1			8	7		2					14
1	3		4	5	6			9	10	11	8				2	7							15
	3		4	5	6	7		9	10	11		1	8		2								16
	3		4	5	6			9	10	11		1	8		2	7							17
	3		4		6	9			10	7		1			8			2	11	5			18
	3		4	5	6	11		8*				1	7		2				12	9	10		19
	3		4	5	6	11						1	7		2				10	9	8		20
	3			5		11				4		1	7*		2		12		10	9	6	8	21
	3			5	6	11			10	4		1			2				9	7	8		22
	3		4	5	6	11				12		1			2			10*	9	7	8		23
	3		4	5	6	11			10*			1			2			12	9	7	8		24
	3		4	5		11			9	10		1						2	7	8	6		25
	3		4	5	12	11			6	10		1						2	9*	7	8		26
	3		4	5		11			10	7		1			9			2		6	8		27
	3		4	5		11			10	7		1			9			2		6	8		28
	3		4	5		11			10	7		1			9			2		6	8		29
	3		4	5		11			10	7		1			9			2		6	8		30
	3		4	5		11			10	7		1			9			2		6	8		31
	3		4	5		11			10	7		1			9			2		6	8		32
	3		4	5		11			10	7		1			9			2		6	8		33
	3		4	5		11			10	9	7	1						2		6	8		34
	3		4	5		11			10	9	7	1						2		6	8		35
	3		4	5		11			10	9		'1			7			2		6	8		36
	3		4	5		11			10	9		1			7			2		6	8		37
	3		4	5		11			10	9		1			7			2		6	8		38
	3		4	5		11			10	9		1			7			2		6	8		39
	3		4	5		11			10	9		1			7			2	12	6*	8		40
	3		4	5		11			10	6		1			7			2		9	8		41
	3		4	5		11			10	7		1			6			2		9	8		42
9	42	1	40	40	22	34	4	14	38	22	20	33	9	5	33	8		31	11	21	24	1	
			,			2				3	2					1	2	1			1		
	2		13		12		1	6	7	2					2				4		4		

1974-75

1	Aug	17	(a)	Manchester C	L	0-4		30,240
2		19	(h)	Luton T	W	2-0	Bonds, Lampard	23,182
3		24	(h)	Everton	L	2-3	Bonds (pen), McDowell	22,486
4		28	(a)	Luton T	D	0-0		16,931
5		31	(a)	Newcastle U	L	0-2		30,780
6	Sep	7	(h)	Sheffield U	L	1-2	Jennings	20,977
7		14	(a)	Tottenham H	L	1-2	Lampard	27,959
8		21	(h)	Leicester C	W	6-2	Gould 2, Jennings 2, Bonds, Robson	21,377
9		25	(h)	Birmingham C	W	3-0	Jennings, Paddon, Robson	25,495
10		28	(a)	Burnley	W	5-3	Robson 2, Bonds, Brooking, Jennings	17,613
11	Oct	5	(h)	Derby Co	D	2-2	Bonds, Robson	32,900
12		12	(a)	Coventry C	D	1-1	Gould	22,519
13		15	(a)	Everton	D	1-1	Gould	31,855
14		19	(h)	Ipswich T	W	1-0	Jennings	33,543
15		26	(a)	Arsenal	L	0-3		41,004
16	Nov	2	(h)	Middlesbrough	W	3-0	Robson, Boam (og), Paddon	28,915
17		9	(a)	Carlisle U	W	1-0	Lampard	14,141
18		16	(h)	Wolverhampton W	W	5-2	Bonds (pen), Brooking, Lampard, Gould, Jennings	31,708
19		23	(a)	Liverpool	D	1-1	Robson	46,346
20		30	(a)	Queen's Park R	W	2-0	Jennings, Paddon	28,356
21	Dec	7	(h)	Leeds U	W	2-1	Gould, Jennings	39,562
22		14	(h)	Manchester C	D	0-0		33,908
23		21	(a)	Chelsea	D	1-1	Gould	34,969
24		26	(h)	Tottenham H	D	1-1	Robson	37,682
25		28	(a)	Stoke C	L	1-2	Holland	33,498
26	Jan	11	(a)	Leeds U	L	1-2	Robson	40,099
27		18	(h)	Queen's Park R	D	2-2	Bonds (pen), Jennings	28,772
28	Feb	1	(h)	Carlisle U	W	2-0	Holland, Jennings	26,805
29		8	(a)	Middlesbrough	D	0-0		29,179
30		19	(h)	Liverpool	D	0-0		40,256
31		22	(a)	Wolverhampton W	L	1-3	Gould	24,791
32		28	(h)	Newcastle U	L	0-1		32,753
33	Mar	15	(h)	Burnley	W	2-1	Robson, Taylor A	28,830
34		18	(a)	Birmingham C	D	1-1	Taylor A	34,000
35		22	(a)	Sheffield U	L	2-3	Gould, Jennings	25,527
36		28	(h)	Stoke C	D	2-2	Brooking, Jennings	29,811
37		29	(h)	Chelsea	L	0-1		31,025
38	May	1	(a)	Leicester C	L	0-3		30,408
39		12	(a)	Derby Co	L	0-1		31,336
40		19	(h)	Coventry C	L	1-2	Holland	27,431
41		26	(a)	Ipswich T	L	1-4	Holland	31,592
42		28	(h)	Arsenal	W	1-0	Paddon	30,195

FINAL LEAGUE POSITION: 13th in Division One

Appearances

Sub. Appearances

Goals

Day	Coleman	Lampard	Bonds	Taylor T	McDowell	Holland	Paddon	Gould	Brooking	Best	Lock	Ayris	Jennings	Robson	Taylor A	Curbishley	Wooler	
1	2*	3	4	5	6	7	8	9	10	11	12							1
1		3	4	5	2	7	8		10	11	6		9					2
1	2	3	4	5	10	7	8	9		11	6							3
1	2	3	4	5	10	7	8	9		11	6							4
1	2	3	4	5	10	7	8	9*		11	6	12						5
1		3	4	5	2	10	8			11	6	7	9					6
1		3	4	5	2	7	8		10	11	6		9					7
1		3	4	5	2	12	8	9	10		6		7*	11				8
1		3	4	5	2		8	9	10		6		7	11				9
1		3	4	5	2		8	9	10		6		7	11				10
1		3	4	5	2*	12	8	9	10		6		7	11				11
1	2	3	4	5			8	9	10		6		7	11				12
1	2	3	4	5			8	9	10		6		7	11				13
1	2	3	4	5			8	9	10		6		7	11				14
1	12	3	4	5	2*		8	9	10		6		7	11				15
1	2	3	4	5			8	9	10		6		7	11				16
1	2	3	4	5			8	9	10		6		7	11				17
1	2	3	4	5			8	9	10		6		7	11				18
1	2	3	4	5			8	9	10		6		7	11				19
1	2	3	4*	5		12	8	9	10		6		7	11				20
1	2	3	4	5	10		8	9			6		7*	11	12			21
1	2	3	4	5	12		8	9	10		6		7*	11				22
1	2	3	4*	5		7	8	9	10	12	6			11				23
1	2	3		5	4		8	9	10		6		7*	11	12			24
1	2	3		5	10	4	8	9		11	6		12	7*				25
1	2	3	4		5	7	8		10	9	6			11				26
1	2*	3	4	5	9		8		10	12	6		7	11				27
1		3	4	5	2	11	8		10*	12	6		7	9				28
1	12	3	4*	5	2	11	8		10	9	6		7					29
1		3	4	5	2	11	8		10		6		7	9				30
1	2*	3		5	4	11	8	12	10		6		7	9				31
1		3		5	2	11*	8	9	10		6		7	4	12			32
1		3	4*	5	2		8	12	10		6		7	11	9			33
1	2	3		5	4		8	7	10		6			11	9			34
1	2	3		5	4		8	11	10		6		7		9			35
1	2	3*		5	4		8	11	10		6	12	7		9			36
1	2			5	3		8	11	10		6	12	7*		9	4		37
1	2			5	3	4		11	10	7	6				9		8	38
1		3	4	5	2	12	8	11	10		6		7		9*			39
1	2	3		5	4		8*	11	10		6		7		9	12		40
1	2	3		5	4			11	10	8	6		7		9			41
1		3	4	5	2	11	8	12	10		6		7*		9			42
42	27	40	31	39	33	18	40	31	36	12	41	2	32	25	11	1	1	
	2				1	4		3			3	1	4		3	1		
			4	7	1	4		4	9	3			13	10	2			

21

1975-76

1	Aug	16	(a)	Stoke C	W	2-1	Gould, Taylor A		23,744
2		19	(a)	Liverpool	D	2-2	Taylor A 2		40,564
3		23	(h)	Burnley	W	3-2	Taylor A 2, Paddon		27,075
4		25	(h)	Tottenham H	W	1-0	Robson		35,914
5		30	(a)	Queen's Park R	D	1-1	Jennings		28,408
6	Sep	6	(h)	Manchester C	W	1-0	Lampard		29,752
7		13	(a)	Leicester C	D	3-3	Bonds, Holland, Lampard		21,413
8		20	(h)	Sheffield U	W	2-0	Best, Taylor T		28,924
9		27	(a)	Wolverhampton W	W	1-0	Paddon		18,455
10	Oct	4	(h)	Everton	L	0-1			31,005
11		11	(h)	Newcastle U	W	2-1	Curbishley, Taylor A		30,400
12		18	(a)	Middlesbrough	L	0-3			25,831
13		25	(h)	Manchester U	W	2-1	Gould, Taylor A		38,528
14	Nov	1	(a)	Birmingham C	W	5-1	Brooking, Pendrey (og), Lampard, Taylor A 2		28,474
15		8	(h)	Coventry C	D	1-1	Robson		29,501
16		15	(a)	Derby Co	L	1-2	Brooking		31,172
17		22	(h)	Middlesbrough	W	2-1	Holland, Jennings		26,914
18		29	(h)	Arsenal	W	1-0	Taylor A		31,012
19	Dec	6	(a)	Norwich C	L	0-1			27,020
20		13	(a)	Burnley	L	0-2			14,907
21		20	(h)	Stoke C	W	3-1	Jennings 3		21,135
22		26	(a)	Aston Villa	L	1-4	Jennings		51,300
23		27	(h)	Ipswich T	L	1-2	Taylor T (pen)		32,741
24	Jan	10	(h)	Leicester C	D	1-1	Taylor A		24,615
25		17	(a)	Manchester C	L	0-3			32,147
26		24	(h)	Queen's Park R	W	1-0	Taylor A		26,677
27		31	(h)	Liverpool	L	0-4			26,741
28	Feb	7	(a)	Tottenham H	D	1-1	Brooking		32,832
29		14	(a)	Coventry C	L	0-2			16,173
30		21	(h)	Derby Co	L	1-2	Brooking		24,941
31		23	(h)	Leeds U	D	1-1	Taylor A		28,025
32		28	(a)	Manchester U	L	0-4			57,240
33	Mar	6	(h)	Birmingham C	L	1-2	Martin (og)		19,868
34		9	(a)	Leeds U	D	1-1	Jennings		26,453
35		13	(a)	Newcastle U	L	1-2	Jennings		32,842
36		20	(a)	Arsenal	L	1-6	Jennings		34,011
37		27	(h)	Norwich C	L	0-1			20,628
38	Apr	3	(h)	Wolverhampton W	D	0-0			16,769
39		10	(a)	Sheffield U	L	2-3	Jennings 2		18,797
40		17	(h)	Aston Villa	D	2-2	Brooking, Robson		21,642
41		19	(a)	Ipswich T	L	0-4			28,217
42		24	(a)	Everton	L	0-2			26,101

FINAL LEAGUE POSITION: 18th in Division One

Appearances

Sub. Appearances

Goals

Day	McDowell	Lampard	Holland	Taylor T	Lock	Taylor A	Paddon	Gould	Brooking	Robson	Jennings	Ayris	Bonds	Best	Coleman	Curbishley	Orhan	McGiven	Wooler	Pike	Ferguson	
1	2	3	4	5	6	7	8	9	10	11												1
1	2	3	4	5	6	7	8	9*	10	11	12											2
1	2	3	4	5	6	7	8		10	11	9*	12										3
1	2	3	4	5	6	7	8		10	11	9											4
1	2	3	4	5	6	7	8		10	11	9											5
1	2	3	4	5	6	7*	8		10	11	9		12									6
1	2	3	7	5	6		8		10	11	9		4									7
1	2	3	11	5	6	9*	8		10		7		4	12								8
1	2	3	11	5	6	7	8		10				4	9								9
1	2	3	11	5	6	12	8		10		7		4	9*								10
1	6	3	7	5		9	8						4	11	2	10						11
1	2	3*	11	5		7	8		10				4	9	6	12						12
1	6	3	4	5		7	8	9	10	11					2							13
1	2	3	9	5		7	8		10	11			4		6							14
1	6		7	5	3	9	8	12	10	11			4*		2							15
1	2	3	9	5	4	7		8*	10	11	12				6							16
1	2		4	5	3	7	8		10	11	9				6							17
1	2	3	9	5	6	7	8			11	10		4									18
1	4	3	11	5	6	7	8		10	9					2							19
1		3	11	5	6	7	8		10		9	12			2	4*						20
1	4	3	9	5	6	7	8			11	10				2							21
1	4	3	9	5	6	7	8			11	10				2							22
1		3	4	5	6	7	8		10	11	9				2*	12						23
1	2	3	4	5	6	7			9		10		8		11							24
1	2	3	4	5	6	7*	8		10		9		12		11							25
1	2	3	4	5		7	8		9		10				6	11						26
1	2	3	4	5		7	8		10	12	9*				6	11						27
1		3	4	5		7	8		10	11	9				2		6					28
1	2	3	4	5		7	8		10	11	9						6					29
1	7	3	4	5			8		10	11	12				2		9*	6				30
1	2	3	4*	5		7	8		10	11	12						9	6				31
1	2			5	3	7*	8		10	11	12		4				9	6				32
1		3		5		7	8			11			4		2	9	10*		6	12		33
1		3		5	6		8			11	9	7*	4		2	10				12		34
1	12	3*		5	6		8			11	9	7	4		2	10						35
1		3		5	6	7			10	11	9		4		2*	8		12				36
1	10	3		5	6		7			11	9		4		2	8						37
1	4	3	7	5	6*		8		10	11	9	12			2							38
1	6	3	7	5			8		10	11*	9	12	4		2							39
	6	3	7	5		4*	8		10	11	9	12			2						1	40
1	6			5			8		10	11		7	2			4	9*	3		12		41
1	6	3	7	5		12	8		10	11*	9		4		2							42
41	36	37	35	42	26	33	39	4	34	33	26	3	17	5	26	12	5	6	1		1	
		1						2	1		1	4	6	1	2		2		1	3		
		3	2	2		13	2	2	5	3	11		1	1	1							

1976-77

1	Aug	21	(a)	Aston Villa	L	0-4		39,012
2		23	(h)	Queen's Park R	W	1-0	Paddon	31,668
3		28	(h)	Leicester C	D	0-0		24,950
4	Sep	4	(a)	Stoke C	L	1-2	Taylor A	19,131
5		11	(h)	Arsenal	L	0-2		31,965
6		18	(a)	Bristol C	D	1-1	Taylor A	28,932
7		25	(h)	Sunderland	D	1-1	Jennings	24,319
8	Oct	2	(a)	Manchester C	L	2-4	Taylor A, Doyle (og)	37,795
9		6	(h)	Leeds U	L	1-3	Jennings	21,909
10		16	(h)	Ipswich T	L	0-2		24,534
11		23	(a)	Everton	L	2-3	McNaught (og), Bonds	23,163
12		30	(a)	West Brom A	L	0-3		19,856
13	Nov	6	(h)	Tottenham H	W	5-3	Robson B, Jennings, Bonds, Brooking, Curbishley	28,997
14		10	(a)	Norwich C	L	0-1		24,762
15		20	(h)	Newcastle U	L	1-2	Robson B	21,624
16		27	(a)	Manchester U	W	2-0	Brooking, Jennings	55,366
17	Dec	4	(h)	Middlesbrough	L	0-1		20,184
18		18	(h)	Liverpool	W	2-0	Brooking, Jennings	24,175
19		27	(a)	Birmingham C	D	0-0		39,978
20	Jan	1	(a)	Tottenham H	L	1-2	Brooking	44,972
21		3	(h)	West Brom A	D	0-0		25,236
22		22	(h)	Aston Villa	L	0-1		27,577
23	Feb	5	(a)	Leicester C	L	0-2		16,201
24		12	(h)	Stoke C	W	1-0	Robson B	20,160
25		19	(a)	Arsenal	W	3-2	Taylor A 2, Jennings	38,221
26		26	(h)	Bristol C	W	2-0	Bonds (pen), Merrick (og)	29,713
27	Mar	5	(a)	Sunderland	L	0-6		35,357
28		12	(h)	Manchester C	W	1-0	Robson B	24,974
29		22	(a)	Ipswich T	L	1-4	Robson B (pen)	27,315
30	Apr	2	(h)	Everton	D	2-2	Robson B 2 (1 pen)	22,518
31		4	(a)	Queen's Park R	D	1-1	Robson B	24,930
32		8	(h)	Birmingham C	D	2-2	Jennings, Pike	28,167
33		9	(a)	Coventry C	D	1-1	Robson B	15,816
34		11	(h)	Norwich C	W	1-0	Pike	27,084
35		16	(a)	Newcastle U	L	0-3		30,967
36		20	(a)	Derby Co	D	1-1	Pike (pen)	21,380
37		26	(a)	Leeds U	D	1-1	Robson B	16,891
38		29	(a)	Middlesbrough	D	1-1	Robson B	16,500
39	May	4	(h)	Coventry C	W	2-0	Robson B, Pike (pen)	25,461
40		7	(h)	Derby Co	D	2-2	Jennings, Pike	32,079
41		14	(a)	Liverpool	D	0-0		55,675
42		16	(h)	Manchester U	W	4-2	Robson B 2, Lampard, Pike	29,311

FINAL LEAGUE POSITION: 17th in Division One

Appearances

Sub. Appearances

Goals

Day	Coleman	Lampard	Bonds	Green	Curbishley	Taylor A	Paddon	Taylor T	Brooking	Holland	McGiven	Jennings	Orhan	Lock	Ayris	Robson B	Robson K	Devonshire	Pike	Otulakowski	Radford	
1	2	3	4	5	6	7	8	9	10	11												1
1	2	3	6	5	4	7	8	9	10	11												2
1	2		6	5		9	8	7	10	4	3	11										3
1	2	3	4	5		9	8	7*	10	11	6	12										4
1	2*	3	4	5		9	8	7	10	11	6		12									5
1	2	3*	4	5		9	8	6	10	7	12	11										6
1	2		4	5		9	8	6	10		11	7		3								7
1	2		4	5		9	8	6	10		7*	11		3	12							8
1	2		4	5		9	8	6	10			7		3	11							9
1	2		4	5		9*	8	6	10			7		3	12	11						10
1		3	2	5*	4		8	6	10			7	12			11	9					11
1		2	4	7			8	5	10				12	3		9	11*	6				12
1		3	2	4				6	10			9		5		11		7	8			13
1	12	3	2	4				6	10			9		5*		11		7	8			14
1		3	2	4				6*	10			9		5		11	12	7	8			15
1		3	6					5	10			9		2		11		7	8	4		16
1		3	6	12				5	10			9*		2		11		7	8	4		17
1		3	6	4				5	10			9		2		11	7				8	18
1		3	6	4				5	10			9		2		11	7				8	19
1		3	6	4				5	10			9		2		11	7		12		8*	20
1		3	6	4				5	10			9		2		11	7	8				21
1		3	6	4	7			5	10			9		2		11			12	8*		22
1		3	2	5		7			10					6		11		9	4	8		23
1		3	2	5		7			10					6		11*	12	9	4	8		24
1		3	2	5		7			10		11			6				9	4	8		25
1		3	2	5		7			10		11			6				9	4	8		26
1		3	2	5					10		11			6			7	9	4	8		27
1		3	2	5*	12				10		11			6		8		9	7	4		28
1		3	2					5	10		11			6		8		9	7	4		29
1		3	2					5	10		11			6		8		9	4		7	30
1		3	2					5	10		11			6		8		9*	4	12	7	31
1	3		2		12			5	10		11			6		8		9*	4		7	32
1		3	2			7		5	10		6	9				11		8	4			33
1		3	2			11		5	10		6					8		9	4		7	34
1		3	2			11*		5	10		6			12		8		9	4		7	35
1		3	2*			11		5	10		6			12		8		9	4		7	36
1	2	3				11		5	10		6					8		9	4		7	37
1		3	2			11		5	10		6			7		8		9	4			38
1		3	2			11		5	10		6					8		9	4		7	39
1		3	2			11		5	10		6*			12		8		9	4		7	40
1		3	2			11		5	10		6			7		8		9	4			41
1		3	2			11		5	10		6					8		9	4		7	42
42	12	36	41	22	8	24	12	36	42	6	15	27	1	25	1	30	7	27	20	10	18	
	1				2	1					1	4	2	1	2			2	1		2	
		1	3		1	5	1		4			8				14		6				

25

1977-78

1	Aug	20	(h)	Norwich C	L	1-3	Robson B (pen)	28,178
2		24	(a)	Leicester C	L	0-1		18,310
3		27	(h)	Manchester C	L	0-1		25,278
4	Sep	3	(a)	Newcastle U	W	3-2	Jennings, Taylor A, Robson B	26,983
5		10	(h)	Queen's Park R	D	2-2	Holland, Lock	26,922
6		17	(a)	Bristol R	L	2-3	Pike, Robson B	21,180
7		24	(h)	Everton	D	1-1	Dobson (og)	25,296
8	Oct	1	(a)	Arsenal	L	0-3		41,245
9		3	(h)	Middlesbrough	L	0-2		26,508
10		8	(h)	Nottingham F	D	0-0		26,126
11		15	(a)	Wolverhampton W	D	2-2	Pike, Robson B	19,366
12		22	(h)	Aston Villa	D	2-2	Hales, Taylor T	26,599
13		29	(a)	Ipswich T	W	2-0	Hales 2	27,308
14	Nov	5	(a)	Coventry C	L	0-1		23,276
15		12	(h)	West Brom A	D	3-3	Devonshire 2, Robson B (pen)	23,601
16		19	(a)	Derby Co	L	1-2	Bonds	23,273
17		26	(h)	Leeds U	L	0-1		26,883
18	Dec	3	(a)	Liverpool	L	0-2		39,659
19		10	(h)	Manchester U	W	2-1	Brooking, Hales	20,759
20		17	(a)	West Brom A	L	0-1		18,868
21		26	(h)	Birmingham C	W	1-0	Curbishley	25,572
22		27	(a)	Chelsea	L	1-2	Robson B	44,093
23		31	(h)	Leicester C	W	3-2	Cross, Hales, McDowell	25,455
24	Jan	2	(a)	Norwich C	D	2-2	Devonshire, Hales	29,480
25		14	(a)	Manchester C	L	2-3	Brooking, Cross	43,627
26		21	(h)	Newcastle U	W	1-0	Hales	25,461
27	Feb	11	(h)	Bristol C	L	1-2	Robson B	19,934
28		18	(a)	Everton	L	1-2	Hales	33,862
29		25	(h)	Arsenal	D	2-2	Cross, Taylor A	31,675
30	Mar	4	(a)	Nottingham F	L	0-2		33,924
31		11	(h)	Wolverhampton W	L	1-2	Hales	23,525
32		14	(a)	Queen's Park R	L	0-1		20,394
33		18	(a)	Aston Villa	L	1-4	Brooking	28,275
34		24	(h)	Ipswich T	W	3-0	Cross 3	23,867
35		25	(h)	Chelsea	W	3-1	Brooking, Green, Holland	24,987
36		28	(a)	Birmingham C	L	0-3		23,554
37	Apr	1	(h)	Coventry C	W	2-1	Holland, Taylor T	19,260
38		8	(a)	Leeds U	W	2-1	Hales, Martin	22,953
39		15	(h)	Derby Co	W	3-0	Robson B 2, Cross	25,424
40		22	(a)	Manchester U	L	0-3		54,089
41		25	(a)	Middlesbrough	W	2-1	Cross 2	13,247
42		29	(h)	Liverpool	L	0-2		37,448

FINAL LEAGUE POSITION: 20th in Division One

Appearances

Sub. Appearances

Goals

Day	Brush	Lampard	Pike	Taylor T	Lock	Taylor A	Robson B	Radford	Brooking	Devonshire	Curbishley	Otulakowski	Holland	Jennings	McGiven	Hales	Bonds	McDowell	Cross	Ferguson	Green	Martin	
1	2	3	4	5	6	7	8	9	10	11													1
1	2	3	4	5	6	7	8	9		11*	10	12											2
1	3	2	4	5	6	7*	8	9		11	10	12											3
1	3	2		5	6	7	8			11	10		4	9									4
1	3	2	7	5	6		8			11	10	12	4	9*									5
1	3	2	12	5	6	7	8		10	11*	9		4										6
1	3	2		5		7	8		10	11	9		4		6								7
1	3	2	12	5		7	8		10	11	9*		4		6								8
1	3	2	11	5		7	8		10	12			4		6	9*							9
1	3	2	11	5			8	9	10	7	4				6								10
1	3	2	6	5			8	9	10	7						11	4						11
1	3	2	6	5			8	9	10	7						11	4						12
1	3	2	6	5			8	9	10	7						11	4						13
1	3	2	6	5			8	9	10	7						11	4						14
1	3	2	6	5			8		10	7	9					11	4						15
1	3	2	6	5			8	9	10	7						11	4						16
1	3	2	6	5			8	9*	10	7	12					11	4						17
1	3	2	6	5*			8		10	7	9		12			11	4						18
1	3	2*	6	5			8		10	7	9					11	4	12					19
1	3		6	5			8		10	7						11	4	2	9				20
1		3	6	5			8		10	7	11						4	2	9				21
1		3	6	5			8		10	7	11						4	2	9				22
		3		5			8		10	7	6					11	4	2	9	1			23
	2	3		5			8		10	7	6					11	4		9	1			24
		3		5			8		10	7	6					11	4	2	9	1			25
		3	8	5		10				7*	6		12			11	4	2	9	1			26
1		3		5		12	8		10	7						11*	4	2	9		6		27
		3	4	5			8		10	7						11	2*	12	9	1	6		28
		3	12	5		11	8		10	7	4							2*	9	1	6		29
		3		5					10	7	4	12	8			11		2	9	1	6*		30
		3		5					10	7	4	12	8			11	6	2*	9	1			31
		3	11	5					10	7	6		8				4	2	9	1			32
		3		5					10	7*	4		8			11	6	2	9	1		12	33
		3	7	5					10		4		8			11	2		9	1	6		34
		3	7	5		11			10		4		8				2		9	1	6		35
		3	7	5		11			10		4		8			12	2		9		6*		36
		3	7*	5		11			10		4		8			9	2			1	6	12	37
		3		5		11			10	7			8				2		9	1	6	4	38
		3	2	5		11			10	7*	12		8						9	1	6	4	39
	12	3		5		11			10	7			8				2		9	1	6	4*	40
		3		5		11			10	7			8				2		9	1	6	4	41
		3		5*		11			10	7	12		8				2		9	1	6	4	42
23	23	40	25	42	6	10	37	10	37	32	31		18	2	4	23	29	12	21	19	13	5	
	1		3			1				2	1	5	3			1						2	
		2	2		1	2	9		3	3	1		3	1		10	1	1	10		1	1	

27

1978-79

1	Aug	19	(h)	Notts Co	W	5-2	Cross 3, Devonshire, Blockley (og)	25,387
2		23	(a)	Newcastle U	W	3-0	Cross, Devonshire, Robson	27,233
3		26	(a)	Crystal Palace	D	1-1	Taylor A	32,611
4	Sep	2	(h)	Fulham	L	0-1		25,778
5		9	(a)	Burnley	L	2-3	Cross 2	12,303
6		16	(h)	Bristol R	W	2-0	Brooking, Robson	22,189
7		23	(h)	Sheffield U	W	2-0	Robson 2 (2 pens)	24,361
8		30	(a)	Sunderland	L	1-2	Cross	23,676
9	Oct	7	(h)	Millwall	W	3-0	Robson 3 (1 pen)	22,210
10		14	(a)	Oldham A	D	2-2	Robson 2	10,143
11		21	(h)	Stoke C	D	1-1	Brooking	27,859
12		28	(a)	Brighton & HA	W	2-1	Robson 2	32,634
13	Nov	4	(h)	Preston NE	W	3-1	Cross, Devonshire, Lampard	23,579
14		11	(a)	Notts Co	L	0-1		11,002
15		18	(h)	Crystal Palace	D	1-1	Bonds	31,245
16		21	(a)	Fulham	D	0-0		26,556
17		25	(a)	Leicester C	W	2-1	Cross 2	16,149
18	Dec	2	(h)	Cambridge U	W	5-0	Robson 2, Bonds, Curbishley, Taylor A	21,379
19		9	(a)	Wrexham	L	3-4	Cross, Lampard, Robson	15,587
20		16	(h)	Charlton A	W	2-0	Cross, Robson	23,833
21		26	(h)	Orient	L	0-2		29,220
22		30	(h)	Blackburn R	W	4-0	Cross, Robson, Taylor A, Curtis (og)	21,269
23	Jan	20	(a)	Bristol R	W	1-0	Robson	12,418
24	Feb	10	(h)	Sunderland	D	3-3	Cross 2, Robson	24,998
25		24	(h)	Oldham A	W	3-0	Holland, Martin, Robson	26,052
26		26	(a)	Luton T	W	4-1	Cross 2, Devonshire, Robson	14,205
27	Mar	3	(a)	Stoke C	L	0-2		24,912
28		10	(h)	Brighton & HA	D	0-0		35,802
29		17	(a)	Preston NE	D	0-0		15,376
30		24	(h)	Newcastle U	W	5-0	McDowell 2, Devonshire, Lampard, Robson	24,650
31		26	(h)	Leicester C	D	1-1	Robson	23,992
32	Apr	2	(a)	Sheffield U	L	0-3		17,720
33		7	(a)	Cambridge U	D	0-0		11,406
34		9	(h)	Luton T	W	1-0	Carr (og)	25,498
35		14	(a)	Orient	W	2-0	Holland, Pike	17,517
36		16	(h)	Cardiff C	D	1-1	Holland	29,058
37		21	(a)	Charlton A	D	0-0		22,816
38		24	(h)	Burnley	W	3-1	Bonds, Pike, Robson	24,139
39		28	(h)	Wrexham	D	1-1	Bonds	28,865
40	May	5	(a)	Blackburn R	L	0-1		7,585
41		11	(a)	Cardiff C	D	0-0		13,140
42		14	(a)	Millwall	L	1-2	Robson	11,917

FINAL LEAGUE POSITION: 5th in Division Two

Appearances

Sub. Appearances

Goals

28

Ferguson	Lampard	Brush	Holland	Taylor T	Bonds	Curbishley	Devonshire	Cross	Brooking	Robson	Taylor A	Pike	McDowell	Martin	Jennings	Day	Parkes	Morgan	Lansdowne	Brignull	
1	2	3	4	5	6	7	8	9	10	11											1
1	2	3	4	5	6	7	8	9	10*	11	12										2
1	2	3	4	5	6	7	8		11	10											3
1	2	3	4	5	6	7		9	11	10*	8		12								4
1	2	3	4	5	6	7	8	9	11				10								5
1	2	3	4	5	6	7	8	9	10	11											6
1	2*	3	4	5	6	7	8		10	11	12		9								7
1		3	4	5	6	7	8	9	10	11			2								8
1	2	3	4	5	6	7	8	9	10	11											9
1	2	3	4	5	6	7*	8	9	10	11	12										10
1		3	4	5	6	7	8	9	10	11			2								11
		3	4	5	6	7	8	9	10	11			2			1					12
	2	3	4	5	6	7	8	9	10	11						1					13
	2	3	4	5	6	7	8	9	10	11						1					14
	2	3	4*	5	6	7	8	9	10	11	12					1					15
	2	3	4	5	6	7	8	9	11	10						1					16
	2	3	4	5	6	7		9	11	10			8			1					17
	2	3	4	5	6	7	8	9	11	10						1					18
	2	3	4	5		7	8	9	11	10			6			1					19
	2	3	4*	5		7	8	9	11	10	12		6			1					20
	2	3		5		7*	8	9	11	10	4		6	12		1					21
	2	3	4				8	9	10	11	7		6	5		1					22
		3	4		6		8	9	10	11	7		2	5		1					23
		3	7	5	6	4	8	9	10	11*			2		12	1					24
		3	7		6	4	8	9	10	11			2	5			1				25
		3	7		6	4	8	9	10	11			2	5			1				26
		3	7		6	4	8	9	10	11			2	5			1				27
	2	3	7		6	4	8	9		11			10	5			1				28
	2	3	7		6		8	9	10	11			4	5			1				29
	2	3	7		6		8	9	10*	11	12		4	5			1				30
	2	3	7		6	12	8	9	11	10			4*	5			1				31
	2	3	7		6		8	9	11	10			4	5			1				32
	2*	3	7	5		4	8	9	11		12		10	6			1				33
		3	7		6	4	8		11	10			2	5			1	9			34
		3	7		6	4	8	9	11	10			2	5			1				35
		3	7		6	4	8	9	11	10			2	5			1				36
	12	3	7		6	4	8	9		10			2	5	11*		1				37
		3	7		6	4	8	9	11	10			2	5			1				38
		3	7		6	4	8	9	11	10*			2	5			1		12		39
	2	3	7		6	4	8	9	11		12		10*	5			1				40
	2	3	7		6	4	8	9					10*	5			1	11		12	41
	2	3	7		6	4	8	9	10	11				5			1				42
11	28	42	39	32	39	26	41	40	21	40	10	10	26	22	2	13	18	2			
1				1							3	4	2		2				1	1	
	3		3		4	1	5	17	2	24	3		2	1							

1979-80

1	Aug	18	(a)	Wrexham	L	0-1			13,036
2		20	(h)	Chelsea	L	0-1			31,627
3		25	(h)	Oldham A	W	1-0	Holland		18,319
4	Sep	1	(a)	Watford	L	0-2			23,329
5		8	(a)	Preston NE	D	1-1	Cross		10,460
6		15	(h)	Sunderland	W	2-0	Cross, Pearson		24,021
7		22	(a)	Queen's Park R	L	0-3			24,692
8		29	(h)	Burnley	W	2-1	Lansdowne, Stewart (pen)		18,327
9	Oct	6	(h)	Newcastle U	D	1-1	Cross		23,206
10		13	(a)	Leicester C	W	2-1	Cross, Martin		22,472
11		20	(h)	Luton T	L	1-2	Allen		25,049
12		27	(a)	Notts Co	W	1-0	Holland		12,256
13	Nov	3	(h)	Wrexham	W	1-0	Pike		20,595
14		10	(a)	Fulham	W	2-1	Cross, Stewart (pen)		16,410
15		14	(a)	Chelsea	L	1-2	Holland		30,859
16		17	(h)	Swansea C	W	2-0	Brooking, Cross		21,210
17		24	(h)	Cardiff C	W	3-0	Stewart 2 (2 pens), Cross		20,292
18	Dec	1	(a)	Charlton A	L	0-1			19,021
19		8	(h)	Bristol R	W	2-1	Cross 2		17,763
20		15	(a)	Shrewsbury T	L	0-3			8,513
21		21	(h)	Cambridge U	W	3-1	Neighbour, Pearson, Stewart		11,721
22	Jan	1	(a)	Orient	W	4-0	Pearson 2, Devonshire, Pike		23,885
23		12	(h)	Watford	D	1-1	Bonds		23,553
24		19	(h)	Preston NE	W	2-0	Allen, Stewart (pen)		17,603
25	Feb	9	(h)	Queen's Park R	W	2-1	Pearson, Hazell (og)		26,037
26		19	(a)	Burnley	W	1-0	Devonshire		10,610
27		23	(h)	Leicester C	W	3-1	Cross, Holland, Pike		27,762
28	Mar	1	(a)	Luton T	D	1-1	Stewart		20,040
29		11	(h)	Notts Co	L	1-2	Pike		24,844
30		15	(a)	Newcastle U	D	0-0			25,431
31		22	(h)	Fulham	L	2-3	Devonshire, Stewart (pen)		30,030
32		29	(a)	Swansea C	L	1-2	Devonshire		13,275
33	Apr	1	(a)	Cambridge U	L	0-2			8,863
34		5	(h)	Orient	W	2-0	Brooking, Gray (og)		22,066
35		7	(a)	Birmingham C	D	0-0			28,377
36		19	(a)	Cardiff C	W	1-0	Stewart		12,076
37		22	(h)	Birmingham C	L	1-2	Martin		37,167
38		26	(h)	Shrewsbury T	L	1-3	Brooking		19,765
39		29	(a)	Oldham A	D	0-0			8,214
40	May	3	(a)	Bristol R	W	2-0	Cross, Devonshire		9,824
41		5	(h)	Charlton A	W	4-1	Cross, Morgan, Pike, Stewart (pen)		19,314
42		12	(a)	Sunderland	L	0-2			45,000

FINAL LEAGUE POSITION: 7th in Division Two

Appearances

Sub. Appearances

Goals

Parkes	Lampard	Brush	Holland	Martin	Bonds	Pike	Devonshire	Cross	Brooking	Pearson	Banton	Morgan	Lansdowne	Stewart	Neighbour	Allen	Ferguson	Smith	
1	2	3	4	5	6	7	8	9	10	11									1
1	2	3	6	5	4	7	11	9	10	8*	12								2
1	2	3	4	5	6	7	8	9	10			11							3
1	2	3	6	5	4	7	11	9	10	8*		12							4
1	2	3	6			4	7		9	10	8	11		5					5
1	2	3		5	4		11	9	10	8				6	7				6
1	2	3	12	5	4	8*	11	9	10					6	7				7
1		3		5	4		11	9	10				8	2	7	6			8
1		3	12	5	4		11	9	10				8	2	7*	6			9
1		3	6	5	4			9	10				8	2	11	7			10
1		3	6	5	4	10		9					8	2	11	7			11
1		3	6	5	4	8		9	10					2	11	7			12
1		3	6	5	4	8	10*	9					12	2	11	7			13
		3	6	5	4	8	10	9						2	11	7	1		14
		3	6	5	4		8	9	10				12	2	11	7*	1		15
1			6	5	4		8	9	10				11	2		7	3		16
1		3	6	5	4		11	9	10	8				2		7			17
1		3	6*	5	4		11	9	10	8				2	12	7			18
1		3		5	4		11	9	10	8				2	7	6			19
1		3		5	4	6		9	10	8				2	11	7			20
1		3		5	4	12	6	9*	10	8				2	11	7			21
1		3		5	4	9	6		10	8				2	11	7			22
1		3		5	4	9	6		10	8				2	11	7			23
1	2	3		5	6*	9	11		10		12			4	7	8			24
1	2	3		5	4		8	9	10	11				6		7			25
1	2	3		5			11	6	9	10				4	8	7			26
1	2	3	8	5			11	6	9	10				4		7			27
1	2	3	8*	5			11	6	9	10	12			4		7			28
1	2*	3	12	5			11	6	9	10	8			4		7			29
1	2	3	12	5			11*	6	9	10	8			4		7			30
1	2	3*	11	5			12	6	9	10	8			4		7			31
1		3	11	5	4	9	6	12	10	8				2		7*			32
1	2	3	11	5	4		6	9	10	8				7					33
1	2*	3	11	5	4	12	6	9	10	8				7					34
1		3	11	5	4		6	9	10	8				2		7			35
1	2	3		5		11	6	9	10	8				4		7			36
1	2	3		5	4	12	6	9	10	8				11		7*			37
1	2	3		5		6		9*	10	11		12		4	7	8			38
1	2	3		5	4	8*		9	10			12		11	7	6			39
1	2			5	4	10	6	9					8	3	11	7			40
1	12	3		5	4	8		9*	10		6	11		2	7				41
1		3	12	5	4	11	6	9	10	8*				2	7				42
40	35	27	21	40	34	27	34	38	37	24	2	4	5	38	22	31	2	1	
	1		5			4		1		1	2	2	3		1				
			4	2	1	5	5	12	3	5			1	1	10	1	2		

1980-81

1	Aug	16	(h)	Luton T	L	1-2	Stewart (pen)	27,933
2		19	(a)	Bristol C	D	1-1	Cross	13,554
3		23	(a)	Preston NE	D	0-0		9,063
4		30	(h)	Notts Co	W	4-0	Goddard 2, Cross, Stewart (pen)	21,769
5	Sep	6	(a)	Chelsea	W	1-0	Wilkins (og)	32,669
6		13	(h)	Shrewsbury T	W	3-0	Cross, Goddard, King (og)	22,339
7		20	(h)	Watford	W	3-2	Barnes, Brooking, Cross	24,288
8		27	(a)	Cambridge U	W	2-1	Cross, Goddard	8,591
9	Oct	4	(a)	Newcastle U	D	0-0		24,848
10		7	(h)	Cardiff C	W	1-0	Neighbour	20,402
11		11	(h)	Blackburn R	W	2-0	Cross 2	32,402
12		18	(a)	Oldham A	D	0-0		8,344
13		25	(h)	Bolton W	W	2-1	Pike, Walsh (og)	25,257
14	Nov	1	(a)	Bristol R	W	1-0	Goddard	6,328
15		8	(h)	Grimsby T	W	2-1	Cross 2	25,468
16		11	(h)	Bristol C	W	5-0	Goddard 2, Brooking, Martin, Cross	25,210
17		15	(a)	Luton T	L	2-3	Brooking 2	17,031
18		22	(h)	Swansea C	W	2-0	Cross, Goddard	27,376
19		26	(a)	Derby Co	L	0-2		18,446
20		29	(a)	Wrexham	D	2-2	Devonshire, Goddard	8,941
21	Dec	6	(h)	Sheffield W	W	2-1	Brooking, Holland	30,476
22		13	(a)	Blackburn R	D	0-0		13,279
23		20	(h)	Derby Co	W	3-1	Brooking, Cross, Goddard	24,071
24		26	(a)	Queen's Park R	L	0-3		23,811
25		27	(h)	Orient	W	2-1	Allen, Holland	34,408
26	Jan	10	(a)	Swansea C	W	3-1	Brooking, Cross, Pike	22,110
27		17	(a)	Notts Co	D	1-1	Holland	13,718
28		31	(h)	Preston NE	W	5-0	Devonshire 2, Pike, Goddard, Lampard	26,413
29	Feb	7	(a)	Shrewsbury T	W	2-0	Cross, Devonshire	9,201
30		14	(h)	Chelsea	W	4-0	Brooking 2, Cross, Devonshire	35,164
31		21	(h)	Cambridge U	W	4-2	Stewart 2 (1 pen), Devonshire, Goddard	36,002
32		28	(a)	Watford	W	2-1	Cross 2	20,786
33	Mar	7	(h)	Newcastle U	W	1-0	Cross	26,274
34		21	(h)	Oldham A	D	1-1	Goddard	24,394
35		28	(a)	Bolton W	D	1-1	Brooking	13,271
36	Apr	4	(h)	Bristol R	W	2-0	Goddard, Pike	23,544
37		11	(a)	Grimsby T	W	5-1	Cross 4, Pike	17,924
38		18	(a)	Orient	W	2-0	Neighbour, Pike	14,592
39		21	(h)	Queen's Park R	W	3-0	Goddard 3	24,599
40	May	2	(h)	Wrexham	W	1-0	Stewart (pen)	30,515
41		6	(a)	Cardiff C	D	0-0		10,558
42		8	(a)	Sheffield W	W	1-0	Morgan	21,087

FINAL LEAGUE POSITION: 1st in Division Two

Appearances

Sub. Appearances

Goals

Parkes	Stewart	Brush	Bonds	Martin	Devonshire	Holland	Goddard	Cross	Brooking	Pike	Lampard	Neighbour	Morgan	Barnes	Allen	Pearson	
1	2	3	4	5	6	7	8*	9	10	11	12						1
1	2	3	4	5	6	7	8	9	10	11							2
1	4	3		5	6	7	8	9	10	11	2						3
1	2		4	5	6	7	8	9	10	11	3						4
1	2		4	5	6	7	8	9	10	11	3						5
1	2		4	5	6		8	9	10	11	3	7*	12				6
1	2		4	5	6		8	9	10	11	3		7				7
1	2		4	5	6	7	8	9	10	11	3						8
1	2	12	4	5	6	7	8*	9		11	3	10					9
1	2		4	5	6	7		9		11	3	10	8				10
1	2		4	5	6	7	8	9		11	3	10					11
1	2		4	5	6*	7		9		11	3	10	8	12			12
1	2	3	4	5	6	7	8	9		11		10					13
1	2	12	4	5	6*	7	8	9		11	3	10					14
1		2	4	5		7	8	9	10	11	3	6					15
1	2		4	5	6	7	8	9	10	11	3						16
1	2		4	5	6	7	8	9	10	11	3						17
1	2		4	5	6*	7	8	9	10	11	3	12					18
1	2		4	5	6	7	8	9	10	11	3						19
1	2		4	5	6	7	8	9	10	11	3						20
1	2		4	5	6	7	8	9	10	11	3						21
1	2		4	5	6	7	8	9	10	11	3						22
1	2		4	5	6	7	8	9	10	11	3						23
1	2		4	5	6	7	8	9*	10	11	3	12					24
1	2		4	5	6	7	8		10	11	3*		9	12			25
1	2		4	5	6	7	8	9	10	11	3						26
1	2	3	4	5	6	7*	8	9	10	11				12			27
1	2		4	5	6		8	9	10	11	3	7					28
1	2		4	5	6		8*	9	10	11	3	7		12			29
1	2		4	5	6		8	9	10	11	3	7					30
1	2		4	5	6		8	9	10	11	3	7					31
1	2		4	5	6		8	9	10	11	3	7					32
1	2		4	5			8	9	10	11	3	7		6*	12		33
1	2	6*	4	5			8	9	10	11	3			12	7		34
1	2		4	5*	6		8	9	10	11	3	7			12		35
1	2	5	4		6		8	9	10	11	3	7					36
1	2		4	5	6		8	9	10	11	3	7					37
1	2		4	5	6			9	10	11	3	7		12	8*		38
1	2		4	5	6			9	10*	11	3	7		12			39
1	2		4	5	6		8*	9	10	11	3	7			12		40
1	2		4	5	6			9	10	11	3	7	8				41
1	2	12	4	5*	6			9	10	11	3	7	8				42
42	41	8	41	41	39	25	37	41	36	42	38	22	5	1	1	2	
		3									1	2	1	5	2	3	
	5			1	6	3	17	22	10	6	1	2	1	1	1		

33

1981-82

1	Aug	29	(h)	Brighton & HA	D	1-1	Stewart (pen)	30,468
2	Sep	2	(a)	Tottenham H	W	4-0	Cross 4	41,200
3		5	(a)	Sunderland	W	2-0	Cross, Goddard	28,347
4		12	(h)	Stoke C	W	3-2	Goddard 2, Stewart (pen)	28,774
5		19	(a)	West Brom A	D	0-0		19,516
6		22	(h)	Southampton	W	4-2	Goddard 3, Pike	34,026
7		26	(h)	Liverpool	D	1-1	Pike	30,802
8	Oct	3	(a)	Birmingham C	D	2-2	Cross 2	22,290
9		10	(h)	Everton	D	1-1	Martin	31,608
10		17	(a)	Aston Villa	L	2-3	Brooking, Cross	32,064
11		24	(a)	Notts Co	D	1-1	Brooking	12,505
12		31	(h)	Middlesbrough	W	3-2	Goddard, Neighbour, Stewart (pen)	27,604
13	Nov	7	(a)	Nottingham F	D	0-0		26,327
14		21	(h)	Coventry C	W	5-2	Martin 2, Brooking, Neighbour, Stewart (pen)	26,065
15		28	(a)	Leeds U	D	3-3	Brooking 2, Cross	25,637
16	Dec	5	(h)	Arsenal	L	1-2	Pearson	33,833
17	Jan	5	(a)	Liverpool	L	0-3		28,427
18		16	(a)	Brighton & HA	L	0-1		22,620
19		27	(a)	Manchester U	L	0-1		41,291
20		30	(h)	West Brom A	W	3-1	Cross 2, Goddard	24,423
21	Feb	2	(h)	Manchester C	D	1-1	Bonds	26,552
22		6	(a)	Stoke C	L	1-2	Van der Elst	11,987
23		13	(h)	Birmingham C	D	2-2	Orr, Stewart (pen)	22,512
24		20	(a)	Southampton	L	1-2	Stewart (pen)	24,026
25		27	(a)	Everton	D	0-0		28,618
26	Mar	2	(h)	Ipswich	W	2-0	Devonshire, Van der Elst	24,846
27		6	(h)	Aston Villa	D	2-2	Stewart (pen), Van der Elst	26,894
28		13	(h)	Notts Co	W	1-0	Stewart (pen)	22,145
29		20	(a)	Middlesbrough	W	3-2	Goddard 2, Van der Elst	12,134
30		27	(h)	Nottingham F	L	0-1		24,633
31		30	(a)	Swansea C	W	1-0	Van der Elst	20,272
32	Apr	3	(a)	Manchester C	W	1-0	Goddard	30,875
33		6	(h)	Wolverhampton W	W	3-1	Goddard 2, Martin	20,651
34		10	(h)	Swansea C	D	1-1	Goddard	26,566
35		13	(a)	Ipswich T	L	2-3	Cross 2	28,767
36		17	(a)	Coventry C	L	0-1		13,398
37		24	(h)	Leeds U	W	4-3	Brooking 2, Cross, Stewart (pen)	24,748
38	May	1	(a)	Arsenal	L	0-2		34,997
39		4	(h)	Sunderland	D	1-1	Stewart (pen)	17,130
40		8	(h)	Manchester U	D	1-1	Cross	26,337
41		10	(h)	Tottenham H	D	2-2	Brooking, Goddard	27,677
42		15	(a)	Wolverhampton W	L	1-2	Cross	13,283

FINAL LEAGUE POSITION: 9th in Division One

Appearances

Sub. Appearances

Goals

Parkes	Stewart	Lampard	Bonds	Martin	Devonshire	Neighbour	Goddard	Cross	Allen	Pike	Pearson	McAlister	Brooking	Brush	Barnes	Banton	Van der Elst	Orr	Cowie	Laronde	Houghton	#
1	2	3	4	5	6	7	8	9	10	11												1
1	2	3	4	5	6	7	8	9	10	11												2
1	2	3	4	5	6	7	8*	9	10	11	12											3
1	2	3	4	5	6	7	8	9	10	11												4
1	2	3	4	5	6	7	8	9	10	11												5
1	2	3	4	5	6	7	8	9	10	11												6
1	2	3	4	5	6	7	8	9	10	11												7
	2	3	4	5	6	7	8	9		11		1	10									8
	2	3	4	5	6	7	8	9		11		1	10									9
	2	3	4	5	6	7*	8	9		11		1	10	12								10
1	2	3	4	5	6		8	9		11			10	7								11
1	2	3	4	5	6	7	8	9		11			10									12
1	2	3		5	6	7	8	9	4*	11			10	12								13
1	2	3	4	5	6	7	8	9		11			10									14
1	2	3	4	5	6	7*	8	9	12	11			10									15
1	2	3	4	5	6			9		11	8		10	7*	12							16
1	2	3	4	5	6*	7		9		11	8		10	12								17
1	2	3	4	5	6*	7	8	9		11			10				12					18
1	8	3*	4	5			12	9		11			10	2			7	6				19
1	2			4	5		8	9		11			10	3			6	7				20
1	2			4	5		8	9		11	12		10	3*			7	6				21
1	2			4	5		8	9		11			10	3			7	6				22
1	5	2	4			12	8	9		11			10	3*			7	6				23
1	2		4			7	8	9		11			10	3			6	5				24
1	2	12	4			7*	8		6	11			10	3			9	5				25
1	2		4		6		8		7	11			10	3			9	5				26
1	2		4		6		8		7	11			10	3			9	5				27
1	2	3	4		6		8	9	7	11							10	5				28
1	2	3	4		6	12	8		7	11*			10				9	5				29
1	2	3	4		6	12	8	9	11*				10				7	5				30
1	2	3		5	6		8	9	11				10				7	4				31
1	2	3		5	6		8	9	11				10				7	4				32
1	2	3		5	6		8	9	11				10				7	4				33
1	2	3*		5	6	12	8	9	11				10				7	4				34
1	2			5	6	11*	8	9	3				10				7	4	12			35
1	2		5*	6			8	9	11				10				7	4	3	12		36
1	2				6		8	9	4	11			10				7	5		3		37
1	2				6			9	4	11			10				7	5	8*	3	12	38
1	2				6		8	9	4	11			10				7	5		3		39
1	2				6		8	9	4	11			10					5	7	3		40
1	2				6		8	9	4	11			10			12		5	7*	3		41
1	2				6		8	9*	4	11			10			12		5	7	3		42
39	42	27	29	28	35	19	38	38	27	34	2	3	34	10	1		21	24	5	6		
		1				4	1		1		2			3	2	1	1		1	1	1	
	10		1	4	1	2	15	16		2	1		8				5	1				

35

1982-83

1	Aug	28	(h)	Nottingham F	L	1-2	Stewart (pen)	23,796
2		31	(a)	Luton T	W	2-0	Bonds, Goddard	13,403
3	Sep	4	(a)	Sunderland	L	0-1		19,239
4		7	(h)	Ipswich T	D	1-1	Lampard	21,963
5		11	(h)	Birmingham C	W	5-0	Clark, Stewart (pen), Goddard, Van der Elst, Martin	18,754
6		18	(a)	West Brom A	W	2-1	Clark, Van der Elst	15,321
7		25	(h)	Manchester C	W	4-1	Clark 2, Goddard, Van der Elst	23,833
8	Oct	2	(a)	Arsenal	W	3-2	Goddard, Martin, Van der Elst	30,484
9		9	(h)	Liverpool	W	3-1	Clark, Martin, Pike	32,500
10		16	(a)	Southampton	L	0-3		19,840
11		23	(a)	Brighton & HA	L	1-3	Devonshire	20,490
12		30	(h)	Manchester U	W	3-1	Goddard, Pike, Stewart (pen)	31,684
13	Nov	6	(a)	Stoke C	L	2-5	Pike, Stewart (pen)	17,589
14		13	(h)	Norwich C	W	1-0	Clark	22,463
15		20	(a)	Tottenham H	L	1-2	Van der Elst	41,960
16		27	(h)	Everton	W	2-0	Bonds, Stevens (og)	21,424
17	Dec	4	(a)	Aston Villa	L	0-1		24,658
18		11	(h)	Coventry C	L	0-3		19,321
19		18	(a)	Notts Co	W	2-1	Dickens, Hunt (og)	8,457
20		27	(h)	Swansea C	W	3-2	Goddard, Stewart (pen), Van der Elst	23,843
21		29	(a)	Watford	L	1-2	Stewart (pen)	24,870
22	Jan	1	(h)	Tottenham H	W	3-0	Cottee, Pike, Stewart (pen)	33,383
23		4	(h)	Luton T	L	2-3	Clark, Cottee	21,435
24		15	(a)	Nottingham F	L	0-1		17,031
25		22	(h)	West Brom A	L	0-1		19,887
26	Feb	5	(a)	Birmingham C	L	0-3		12,539
27		26	(h)	Southampton	D	1-1	Lampard	19,626
28	Mar	5	(h)	Brighton & HA	W	2-1	Cottee, Dickens	16,850
29		12	(a)	Liverpool	L	0-3		28,551
30		19	(h)	Stoke C	D	1-1	Bould (og)	16,466
31		22	(a)	Manchester U	L	1-2	Devonshire	30,277
32		26	(a)	Norwich C	D	1-1	Dickens	18,582
33	Apr	2	(h)	Watford	W	2-1	Swindlehurst, Van der Elst	22,647
34		5	(a)	Swansea C	W	5-1	Dickens 2, Pike 2, Devonshire	13,303
35		9	(h)	Sunderland	W	2-1	Dickens, Goddard	20,053
36		16	(a)	Manchester C	L	0-2		23,015
37		23	(h)	Aston Villa	W	2-0	Bonds, Swindlehurst	21,822
38		30	(a)	Everton	L	0-2		16,355
39	May	3	(a)	Ipswich T	W	2-1	Goddard, Stewart (pen)	18,690
40		7	(h)	Notts Co	W	2-0	Goddard, Van der Elst	17,534
41		10	(h)	Arsenal	L	1-3	Van der Elst	28,930
42		14	(a)	Coventry C	W	4-2	Cottee 2, Goddard, Swindlehurst	10,919

FINAL LEAGUE POSITION: 8th in Division One

Appearances

Sub. Appearances

Goals

Parkes	Stewart	Lampard	Bonds	Martin	Devonshire	Van der Elst	Goddard	Clarke	Allen	Pike	Neighbour	Morgan	Orr	Brush	Gallagher	Dickens	Cottee	Cowie	Swindlehurst	Brooking	
1	2	3	4	5	6	7	8	9	10	11											1
1	2	3	4	5	6	7	8	9	10		11*	12									2
1	2	3	4	5	6	7	8	9	10	11											3
1	2	3	4	5	6	7	8	9	10	11											4
1	2	3	4	5	6	7	8	9	10	11											5
1	2	3	4	5	6	7	8	9	10	11											6
1	2*	3	4	5	6	7	8	9	10	11		12									7
1	2	3	4	5	6	7*	8	9	10	11		12									8
1	2	3	4*	5	6		8	9	10	11	7	12									9
1	2	3	4	5	6	7	8	9	10	11											10
1	2	3	4	5	6	7	8	9	10	11											11
1	2	3	4	5	6	7	8	9	10	11											12
1	2		4	5	6	7*	8	9	10	11		12	3								13
1	2	3	4	5	6	7	8	9	10	11											14
1	2	3	4	5		7	8	9	10	11	6										15
1	2	3	4	5	6*	7	8	9	10	11		12									16
1	2	3		5		7	8	9	10	11			4	6							17
1	2	3		6*	7	8			10	11		12	4	9	5						18
1		2				7	8	9	10	11			4	3	5	6					19
1	2			5	6	7	8	9	10	11			4	3							20
1	2	3		5	6	7	8	9	10	11					4						21
1	2			5	6	7		9	10	11					3	4	8				22
1	2		5*	6	7		9	10	11			12			3	4	8				23
1	2*	3	4	5	6	7	8	9	10	11					12						24
1		2	4	5	6	7*	8	9	10	11					3		12				25
1		2	4	5	6	7	8	9	10*						3	12		11			26
1	2	3	4	5	6	7	8	9*	10	11						12					27
1	2*	3		5	6	7			10	11	8				4	12	9				28
1	2	3	4	5	6	7	9		10	11	8										29
1	2	3	4	5	6	7	8		10	11	9										30
1	2	3	4	5	6	7	8		10	11		9*				12					31
1	2	3	4	5	6		8			11		7				10			9		32
1	2	3	4	5	6	7	8			11						10	12		9*		33
1	2	3	4	5	6	7	8			11		9				10					34
1	2	3	4	5	6	7	8			11						10	12		9*		35
1	2	3	4		6	7	8*		9	11			5			10	12				36
1	2	3*	4	5	6	7	8			11		12				10			9		37
1	2		4	5	6	7	8			11				3		10			9		38
1	2	3	4	5	6	7	8			11						10			9		39
1	2	3	4	5	6	7	8			11						10			9		40
1	2	3	4	5	6	7	8			11								10	9		41
1	2	3	4		6	7	8		10	11*			5				12		9		42
42	39	37	34	38	39	40	39	26	33	40	3	3	9	6	8	12	3	1	9	1	
													4	5	1	3	5	1			
	8	2	3	3	3	9	10	7		6						6	5		3		

37

1983-84

1	Aug	27	(h)	Birmingham C	W	4-0	Cottee 2, Martin, Swindlehurst		19,729
2		29	(a)	Everton	W	1-0	Walford		20,375
3	Sep	3	(a)	Tottenham H	W	2-0	Swindlehurst, Whitton		38,042
4		6	(h)	Leicester C	W	3-1	Cottee, Swindlehurst, Walford		22,131
5		10	(h)	Coventry C	W	5-2	Swindlehurst 3, Whitton 2		22,195
6		17	(a)	West Brom A	L	0-1			15,161
7		24	(h)	Notts Co	W	3-0	Brooking, Goddard, Stewart (pen)		20,613
8	Oct	1	(a)	Stoke C	L	1-3	Stewart (pen)		13,852
9		15	(h)	Liverpool	L	1-3	Devonshire		32,555
10		22	(h)	Norwich C	D	0-0			18,958
11		29	(a)	Watford	D	0-0			14,559
12	Nov	5	(h)	Ipswich T	W	2-1	Swindlehurst 2		20,682
13		12	(a)	Wolverhampton W	W	3-0	Brooking, Cottee, Swindlehurst		12,062
14		19	(a)	Sunderland	W	1-0	Swindlehurst		19,921
15		27	(h)	Manchester U	D	1-1	Swindlehurst		23,355
16	Dec	3	(a)	Aston Villa	L	0-1			21,297
17		10	(h)	Arsenal	W	3-1	Brooking, Pike, Whyte (og)		25,118
18		17	(a)	Nottingham F	L	0-3			14,544
19		26	(h)	Southampton	L	0-1			22,221
20		27	(a)	Luton T	W	1-0	Cottee		16,343
21		30	(h)	Tottenham H	W	4-1	Brooking, Cottee, Stewart, Martin		30,939
22	Jan	2	(a)	Notts Co	D	2-2	Swindlehurst, Stewart (pen)		8,667
23		14	(a)	Birmingham C	L	0-3			10,334
24		21	(h)	West Brom A	W	1-0	Cottee		17,213
25	Feb	4	(h)	Stoke C	W	3-0	Barnes, Cottee, Stewart (pen)		18,775
26		7	(h)	Queen's Park R	D	1-1	Cottee		20,102
27		11	(a)	Coventry C	W	2-1	Cottee, Bamber (og)		13,271
28		21	(h)	Watford	L	2-4	Barnes, Swindlehurst		19,241
29		25	(a)	Norwich C	L	0-1			16,294
30	Mar	3	(a)	Ipswich T	W	3-0	Cottee, Hilton, Butcher (og)		17,297
31		10	(h)	Wolverhampton W	D	1-1	Cottee		18,111
32		17	(a)	Leicester C	L	1-4	Stewart (pen)		13,533
33		31	(h)	Queen's Park R	D	2-2	Cottee, Pike		21,099
34	Apr	7	(a)	Liverpool	L	0-6			38,359
35		14	(h)	Sunderland	L	0-1			16,558
36		17	(h)	Luton T	W	3-1	Cottee 2, Martin		15,430
37		21	(a)	Southampton	L	0-2			20,846
38		28	(a)	Manchester U	D	0-0			44,124
39	May	5	(h)	Aston Villa	L	0-1			17,393
40		7	(a)	Arsenal	D	3-3	Whitton 2, Hilton		33,347
41		12	(h)	Nottingham F	L	1-2	Stewart (pen)		18,468
42		14	(h)	Everton	L	0-1			25,452

FINAL LEAGUE POSITION: 9th in Division One

Appearances

Sub. Appearances

Goals

Parkes	Stewart	Walford	Bonds	Martin	Devonshire	Whitton	Cottee	Swindlehurst	Brooking	Pike	Orr	Goddard	Dickens	Allen	Lampard	Donald	Brush	Barnes	Hilton	
1	2	3	4	5	6	7	8	9	10*	11	12									1
1	2	3	4	5	6	7	8	9		11	10									2
1	2	3	4	5	6	7	8	9	10	11										3
1	2	3	4	5	6	7	8	9	10	11										4
1	2	3	4	5	6	7	8	9	10	11										5
1	2	3	4	5	6		8	9	10	11	7*	12								6
1	2	3	4	5	6		8	9	10	11	7									7
1	2	3	4	5	6	7		9	10	11	8									8
1	2	3	4	5	6	7	12	9	10	11	8*									9
1	2	3	4	5	6	7*	8	9	10	11		12								10
1	2	3	4	5	6		8	9	10		11		7							11
1	2	3	4*	5	6		8	9		11	7		10	12						12
1	2	4		5	6		8	9	10	11	7				3					13
1	2	4		5	6	7	8	9	10	11					3					14
1	2	4		5	6	7	8	9	10	11					3					15
1	2	4		5	6	7	12	9	10	11	8*				3					16
1	2	4		5	6	7		9	10	11	8				3					17
1	2	4		5	6	7		9	10	11*	8		12		3					18
1	2	4		5	6	7		9	10		8		11		3*	12				19
1	2	4		5	6	7		9	10		8				3			11		20
1	2	4		5	6	7	8	9	10	11					3					21
1	2	4		5	6	7	8	9	10	11					3					22
1	2	4		5		7	8	9	10	11					3			6		23
1	2	4					8	9	10	11	5				3			6	7	24
1	2	4					8	9	10	11	5				3			6	7	25
1	2	4					8	9	10	11	5				3			6	7	26
1	2	4					8	9	10	11	5				3			6	7	27
1	2	5	4				8	9	10	11					3		7	6		28
1	2	5	4				8	9	10	11					3		7	6		29
1	2	5	4				8	9	10	11	7				3			6		30
1	2	5	4				8	9	10		6	12		11	3			7*		31
1	2	5	4				8	9	10	11	6*			7	3			12		32
1	2	3	4	5			8	9	10	11	6			7						33
1	2	3	4	5			8	9	10	11	6			7						34
1	2		4	5			8	9	10	11	6*			7	3			12		35
1	2	3	4	5			8	9	10	11				7				6		36
1	2	3	4	5			8	9	10	11				7				6*	12	37
1	2	3	4	5			8	9	10	11				7				6		38
1	2*	3	4				8	9	10	11	6		12	7				5		39
1	2	5	4				8	9	10	11				7	3			6		40
1	2	5	4				8	9	10	11			12	7	3*			6		41
1	2	5	4				8	9	10	11*			12	7	3			6		42
42	42	41	27	29	22	22	37	35	35	27	28	3	7	19	17	1	10	11	7	
							2	1		1	1	2	3		1	1		2	1	
	7	2		3	1	5	15	13	4	2		1						2	2	

1984-85

No	Month	Date		Opponent	Result	Score	Scorers	Attendance
1	Aug	25	(h)	Ipswich T	D	0-0		19,032
2		27	(a)	Liverpool	L	0-3		32,633
3	Sep	1	(a)	Southampton	W	3-2	Goddard 2, Dickens	18,488
4		4	(h)	Coventry C	W	3-1	Stewart 2 (2 pens), Cottee	14,949
5		8	(h)	Watford	W	2-0	Barnes, Sinnott (og)	20,377
6		15	(a)	Chelsea	L	0-3		32,411
7		22	(h)	Nottingham F	D	0-0		17,434
8		29	(a)	Newcastle U	D	1-1	Allen	29,452
9	Oct	6	(h)	Leicester C	W	3-1	Bonds, Cottee, Stewart (pen)	15,306
10		13	(a)	Manchester U	L	1-5	Goddard	47,559
11		20	(a)	Stoke C	W	4-2	Allen, Cottee, Goddard, Berry (og)	9,945
12		27	(h)	Arsenal	W	3-1	Cottee, Goddard, Pike	33,218
13	Nov	3	(a)	Aston Villa	D	0-0		15,709
14		10	(h)	Everton	L	0-1		24,089
15		17	(h)	Sunderland	W	1-0	Cottee	15,204
16		24	(a)	Luton T	D	2-2	Martin, Whitton	10,789
17	Dec	1	(h)	West Brom A	L	0-2		15,572
18		8	(a)	Norwich C	L	0-1		13,908
19		15	(h)	Sheffield W	D	0-0		14,896
20		22	(h)	Southampton	L	2-3	Cottee 2	14,221
21		26	(a)	Tottenham H	D	2-2	Cottee, Goddard	37,198
22		29	(a)	Coventry C	W	2-1	Cottee 2	10,775
23	Jan	1	(h)	Queen's Park R	L	1-3	Brush	20,857
24	Feb	2	(h)	Newcastle U	D	1-1	Allen	17,723
25		23	(h)	Aston Villa	L	1-2	Goddard	14,845
26	Mar	2	(a)	Arsenal	L	1-2	Cottee	25,818
27		15	(h)	Manchester U	D	2-2	Stewart (pen), Duxbury (og)	16,674
28		23	(a)	Leicester C	L	0-1		11,375
29		30	(a)	Nottingham F	W	2-1	Cottee, Goddard	13,560
30	Apr	2	(a)	Watford	L	0-5		17,884
31		6	(h)	Tottenham H	D	1-1	Dickens	24,435
32		8	(a)	Queen's Park R	L	2-4	Cottee 2	16,085
33		13	(h)	Chelsea	D	1-1	Cottee	19,003
34		20	(a)	Sunderland	W	1-0	Goddard	15,622
35		2	(h)	Luton T	D	0-0		17,303
36	May	4	(a)	West Brom A	L	1-5	Stewart (pen)	8,878
37		6	(h)	Norwich C	W	1-0	Barnes	16,223
38		8	(a)	Everton	L	0-3		32,657
39		11	(a)	Sheffield W	L	1-2	Cottee	24,314
40		14	(h)	Stoke C	W	5-1	Bonds 2, Hilton, Pike, Stewart (pen)	13,362
41		17	(a)	Ipswich T	W	1-0	Cottee	19,296
42		20	(h)	Liverpool	L	0-3		22,408

FINAL LEAGUE POSITION: 16th in Division One

Appearances

Sub. Appearances

Goals

McAlister	Stewart	Walford	Allen	Martin	Gale	Whitton	Cottee	Goddard	Dickens	Pike	Hilton	Barnes	Bonds	Swindlehurst	Campbell	Orr	Brush	Potts	Parkes	McPherson	Lampard	Parris	
1	2	3	4	5	6	7*	8	9	10	11	12												1
1	2	3	4	5	6		12	9		11		7	8	10*									2
1	2	3	4	5	6		9	8*	10	11	12	7											3
1	2	3	4	5	6		9		10	11		7*	12			8							4
1	2	3	4	5	6		9		10	11		7	12			8*							5
1	2	3	4	5*	6		9	12	10	11		7	8										6
1	2	3	4		6		9	8	10	11		7	5										7
1	2	3	4	5	6		9	8		11		7	10										8
1	2	3	4	5	6	12	9	8		11		7*	10										9
1	2	3	4	5	6	7	9	8		11			10										10
1	2	3	4	5	6	7	9	8		11*			10			12							11
1	2	3	4	5	6	7	9	8		11			10										12
1	2	3	4	5	6*	7	9	8		11			10			12							13
1	2	3	4	5	6*	7	9	8	12	11			10										14
1	2	3	4	5	6	7	9	8		11			10										15
1	2	3*	4	5	6	7	9	8		11			10	12									16
1	2	3	4	5	6	7	9	8		11			10*	12									17
1	2	3	4	5	6	7	9	8	10	11*	12												18
1		3	2	5	6	7	10	8	4	11				9									19
1		3	2	5	6	7	10	8	4*	11				9		12							20
1			2	5	6		10	12	4	11	8			9*		7	3						21
1			2	5	6	12	10	9	4	11	8*					7	3						22
1			7	5	6*	12	10	9	4		8					11	3	2					23
1	2	6	7	5			10	9	4	11		8					3						24
1	2	4	7	5			10	9	6	11		8*		12			3						25
1	2	6	7	5			10	9	4	11						8	3						26
1	2	4	7	5			10	9	11*		6			12		8	3						27
1	2	4	7	5	6		10	9	11*					12		8	3						28
1	2	3	4	5	6		8	9*		10		11		12		7							29
1	2	4	7	5	6		10	9		11*		8		12			3						30
1	2	4	7	5	6		10	9	11			8*		12			3						31
1*	2	4	7	5	6		10	9	11			12		8			3						32
	2	4	7		6		10	9	11					8		5	3		1				33
	2		7	5	6		10	9	11					8		4	3		1				34
	2		7	5	6		10	9	11				12	8*		4	3		1				35
	2		7	5	6	8	10	9	11				4				3		1				36
	2		7	5	6		9	10	11*			12	8			4	3		1				37
	2		7	5	6		10	9				11	8			4	3		1				38
	2	7*		5	6	12	10	9				11	8			4	3		1				39
	2			5	4		10	11		6	12	9	8			7*	3		1				40
	2	4		5			10	9		11	6	7	8				3		1				41
	2	10		5	12			9		11		7					3		1	4	6*	8	42
32	37	33	38	40	36	13	40	38	24	30	5	18	19	8	2	17	18	1	10	1	1	1	
						1	4	1	2	1		4	2	3	8	3							
		6	3	1		1	17	9	2	2	1	2	3				1						

1985-86

1	Aug	17	(a)	Birmingham C	L	0-1		11,164
2		20	(h)	Queen's Park R	W	3-1	McAvennie 2, Dickens	15,530
3		24	(h)	Luton T	L	0-1		14,104
4		26	(a)	Manchester U	L	0-2		50,773
5		31	(h)	Liverpool	D	2-2	McAvennie 2	19,762
6	Sep	3	(a)	Southampton	D	1-1	McAvennie	14,477
7		7	(a)	Sheffield W	D	2-2	Cottee, McAvennie	19,287
8		14	(h)	Leicester C	W	3-0	Cottee, Devonshire, McAvennie	12,125
9		21	(a)	Manchester C	D	2-2	Cottee, McCarthy (og)	22,001
10		28	(h)	Nottingham F	W	4-2	McAvennie 2, Cottee, Dickens	14,540
11	Oct	5	(a)	Newcastle U	W	2-1	Cottee, McAvennie	26,709
12		12	(h)	Arsenal	D	0-0		24,057
13		19	(h)	Aston Villa	W	4-1	Cottee 2, McAvennie 2	15,034
14		26	(a)	Ipswich T	W	1-0	Cottee	16,849
15	Nov	2	(h)	Everton	W	2-1	McAvennie 2	23,844
16		9	(a)	Oxford U	W	2-1	Cottee, Ward	13,140
17		16	(h)	Watford	W	2-1	McAvennie, Ward	21,490
18		23	(a)	Coventry C	W	1-0	McAvennie	11,042
19		30	(h)	West Brom A	W	4-0	Cottee, Devonshire, Orr, Parris	16,325
20	Dec	7	(a)	Queen's Park R	W	1-0	McAvennie	23,836
21		14	(h)	Birmingham C	W	2-0	McAvennie, Stewart (pen)	17,481
22		21	(a)	Luton T	D	0-0		14,599
23		26	(a)	Tottenham H	L	0-1		33,835
24	Jan	11	(a)	Leicester C	W	1-0	McAvennie	11,359
25		18	(a)	Liverpool	L	1-3	Dickens	41,056
26	Feb	2	(h)	Manchester U	W	2-1	Cottee, Ward	22,642
27	Mar	15	(a)	Arsenal	L	0-1		31,240
28		19	(a)	Aston Villa	L	1-2	Hunt (og)	11,567
29		22	(h)	Sheffield W	W	1-0	McAvennie	16,604
30		29	(a)	Chelsea	W	4-0	Cottee 2, Devonshire, McAvennie	29,955
31		31	(h)	Tottenham H	W	2-1	Cottee, McAvennie	27,497
32	Apr	2	(a)	Nottingham F	L	1-2	Cottee	17,498
33		8	(h)	Southampton	W	1-0	Martin	22,459
34		12	(h)	Oxford U	W	3-1	McAvennie, Stewart (pen), Trewick (og)	23,956
35		15	(h)	Chelsea	L	1-2	Cottee	29,361
36		19	(a)	Watford	W	2-0	Cottee, McAvennie	16,651
37		21	(h)	Newcastle U	W	8-1	Martin 3 (1 pen), Goddard, McAvennie, Orr, Stewart, Roeder (og)	24,735
38		26	(h)	Coventry C	W	1-0	Cottee	27,251
39		28	(h)	Manchester C	W	1-0	Stewart (pen)	27,153
40		30	(h)	Ipswich T	W	2-1	Dickens, Stewart (pen)	31,121
41	May	3	(a)	West Brom A	W	3-2	Cottee, McAvennie, Stewart (pen)	17,651
42		5	(a)	Everton	L	1-3	Cottee	40,073

FINAL LEAGUE POSITION: 3rd in Division One

Appearances

Sub. Appearances

Goals

Parkes	Stewart	Walford	Gale	Martin	Devonshire	Ward	McAvennie	Goddard	Cottee	Orr	Dickens	Campbell	Parris	Barnes	Potts	Pike	Hilton	
1	2	3	4	5	6	7	8	9*	10	11	12							1
1	2	3	4	5	6	7	8		10	11	9							2
1	2	3	4	5	6	7	8		10*	11	9	12						3
1	2	3	4	5	6	7	8		10*	11	9	12						4
1	2	3	4	5	6	7	8		10	11	9							5
1	2	3	4	5	6	7	8		12	11	9	10*						6
1	2	3	4	5		7	8*		10	11	9		6	12				7
1	2	3	4	5	6	7	8		10	11	9							8
1	2	3	4	5	6	7	8		10	11	9							9
1	2	3	4	5	6	7	8		10	11	9							10
1	2	3	4	5	6	7	8		10	11	9							11
1	2	3	4	5	6	7	8		10	11	9*		12					12
1	2	3	4	5	6	7	8		10	11			9					13
1		3	4	5	6*	7	8		10	11	9		2	12				14
1	2	3*	4	5	6	7	8		10	11	9		12					15
1	2	3	4	5	6	7	8		10	11	9							16
1	2	3	4	5	6	7	8		10	11	9							17
1	2	3	4	5	6	7	8		10	11	9							18
1	2	3	4	5	6	7			10	11	9		8					19
1	2	3	4	5	6	7	8		10	11	9							20
1	2	3*	4	5	6	7	8		10	11	9		12					21
1	2	3	4	5	6	7	8		10	11	9							22
1	2	3	4	5	6	7	8		10	11	9							23
1	2	3	4	5	6	7	8		10		9		11					24
1	2	3	4	5	6	7	8		10		9		11					25
1		3	4	5	6	7	8		10		9		2		11			26
1	2		4	5	6	7	8		10		9		3		11			27
1		3	4	5		7	8	12	10*	6	9		2		11			28
1	2		4	5		7	8	12	10*	6	9		3		11			29
1	2		4		6*	7	8		10	12	9		3		11	5		30
1	2		4		6	7*	8		10	12	9		3		11	5		31
1	2		4	5		7	8		10	6	9		3		11			32
1	2		4	5	6	7	8		10		9		3		11			33
1	2		4	5	6	7	8		10		9		3		11			34
1	2		4*	5	6	7	8		10	12	9		3		11			35
1	2		4	5	6	7	8		10	11	9		3					36
1	2		4	5	6	7	8	12	10	11	9*		3					37
1	2		4	5	6	7	8		10	11	9		3					38
1	2		4	5	6	7	8		10	11	9		3					39
1	2		4	5	6	7	8	12	10	11*	9		3					40
1	2		4	5	6	7	8		10	11	9		3					41
1	2		4	5	6	7	8	12	10	11	9*		3					42
42	39	27	42	40	38	42	41	1	41	33	40	1	23		10	2		
								5	1	3	1	2	3	1	1			
	6			4	3	3	26	1	20	2	4		1					

1986-87

1	Aug	23	(h)	Coventry C	W	1-0	Gale		21,368
2		25	(a)	Manchester U	W	3-2	Devonshire, McAvennie 2		43,306
3		30	(a)	Oxford U	D	0-0			11,684
4	Sep	2	(h)	Nottingham F	L	1-2	McAvennie		21,305
5		6	(h)	Liverpool	L	2-5	Cottee, Stewart (pen)		29,807
6		13	(a)	Queen's Park R	W	3-2	Cottee 3		19,257
7		20	(h)	Luton T	W	2-0	Parris, Gale		19,133
8		27	(a)	Sheffield W	D	2-2	Martin, Orr		25,715
9	Oct	4	(a)	Watford	D	2-2	McAvennie, Dickens		17,120
10		11	(h)	Chelsea	W	5-3	Stewart 2 (2 pens), McAvennie, Cottee 2		26,859
11		18	(a)	Norwich C	D	1-1	Goddard		22,884
12		25	(h)	Charlton A	L	1-3	Cottee		24,141
13	Nov	2	(h)	Everton	W	1-0	Dickens		19,094
14		8	(a)	Arsenal	D	0-0			36,084
15		15	(a)	Wimbeldon	W	1-0	Cottee		10,342
16		22	(h)	Aston Villa	D	1-1	Cottee		21,959
17		30	(a)	Newcastle U	L	0-4			22,077
18	Dec	6	(h)	Southampton	W	3-1	Devonshire, Ince, Cottee (pen)		18,111
19		13	(a)	Manchester C	L	1-3	Martin		19,067
20		20	(h)	Queen's Park R	D	1-1	Cottee (pen)		17,290
21		26	(a)	Tottenham H	L	0-4			39,019
22		27	(h)	Wimbledon	L	2-3	Hilton, Cottee		19,122
23	Jan	1	(h)	Leicester C	W	4-1	McAvennie, Dickens, Cottee 2		16,625
24		3	(a)	Liverpool	L	0-1			41,286
25		24	(a)	Coventry C	W	3-1	Cottee 3		14,191
26	Feb	7	(h)	Oxford U	L	0-1			15,220
27		14	(a)	Nottingham F	D	1-1	Stewart (pen)		19,373
28		28	(a)	Luton T	L	1-2	Cottee		11,101
29	Mar	7	(a)	Charlton A	L	1-2	Robson		10,100
30		14	(h)	Norwich C	L	0-2			21,531
31		21	(a)	Chelsea	L	0-1			25,386
32		24	(h)	Sheffield W	L	0-2			13,514
33		28	(h)	Watford	W	1-0	Parris		16,485
34	Apr	8	(h)	Arsenal	W	3-1	Cottee 2 (1 pen), Brady		26,174
35		11	(a)	Everton	L	0-4			35,731
36		14	(h)	Manchester U	D	0-0			23,486
37		18	(a)	Leicester C	L	0-3			10,434
38		20	(h)	Tottenham H	W	2-1	Cottee (pen), McAvennie		23,972
39		25	(a)	Aston Villa	L	0-4			13,584
40	May	2	(h)	Newcastle U	D	1-1	Ward		17,844
41		4	(a)	Southampton	L	0-1			16,810
42		9	(h)	Manchester C	W	2-0	Cottee, Brady		18,413

FINAL LEAGUE POSITION: 15th in Division One

Appearances

Sub. Appearances

Goals

Parkes	Stewart	Parris	Gale	Martin	Devonshire	Ward	McAvennie	Dickens	Cottee	Orr	Hilton	Goddard	Pike	Keen	Walford	Bonds	Ince	Potts	Robson	Brady	Strodder	McQueen	McAlister	Dolan	#
1	2	3	4	5	6	7	8	9	10	11															1
1	2	3		5	6	7	8	9	10	11	4														2
1	2	3	4	5	6	7	8	9	10	11															3
1	2	3	4	5	6*	7	8	9	10	11		12													4
1	2	3	4	5		7	8	9	10	11			6*	12											5
1	2	3	4	5			8	9	10	11				7	6										6
1	2	6	4	5			8	9*	10	11			12	7	3										7
1	2	3	4	5		7	8	9	10	11					6										8
1	2	3	4*			7	8	9	10	11	5		12	6											9
1	2	3	4			7	8*	9	10	11	5			6		12									10
1	2	3	4		7*			9	10	11	5	8		6		12									11
1	2	3	4		6*	7		9	10	11	5	8		12											12
1	2	3	4		6	7		9	10	11	5	8													13
1	2	3	4		6	7	8	9	10		5				11										14
1	2	3	4		6*	7	8	9	10	11	5				12										15
1		3	4		6	7	8	9	10		5			11*	2	12									16
1	2	3	4		6	7	8	9*	10	11	5				12										17
1		3	4	5	6	7	8		10	11						9		2							18
1		3	4	5	6	7	8	12	10	11*						9		2							19
1		3	4	5	6	7	8	9	10	11								2							20
1		3		5	6	7	8	9	10	11	12			4*				2							21
1		3		5		7	8	12	10		4		11	9*		6		2							22
1		3		5	6	7	8	9	10		4		11					2							23
1		3		5	6		8	9*	10	7	4		11		12			2							24
1		3		5	6	7	8	9	10		4							2	11						25
1	2	3	4		6	7	8	9*	10		5					12			11						26
1	2	3	4			7	8		10				9	6	5				11						27
1	2		4			7	8	6	10				9	3*	5		12		11						28
1	2	12	4			7	8*	6	10				9	3	5				11						29
1	2	3	4					6	10				9*	12	5	8			11	7					30
1	2	3	4			7	8		10				9						11	6	5				31
1	2*	3	4			7	8	9	10				12						11	6	5				32
1		9	4			7	8	12	10							2			11*	6	5	3			33
		9	4			7	8		10							2			11	6	5	3	1		34
		9	4*				8		10			12		7		2			11	6	5	3	1		35
		2				7	8	9	10							4			11	6	5	3	1		36
		9*	4			7	8	12	10							2			11	6	5	3	1		37
			4		6	7	8		10							2			11	9	5	3	1		38
			4		6	7	8	12	10							2*			11	9	5	3	1		39
						7	8	9	10					12		4	6	2	11		5	3*	1		40
						7	8		10							2	6	4	11	9	5	3	1		41
						7*	8		10	3				4			11	2	9	6	5		1	12	42
33	23	35	32	16	20	37	36	31	42	21	15	3	10	7	13	13	7	8	18	12	12	9	9		
		1						5		1	1	1	1	6	1	4	3							1	
	4	2	2	2	2	1	7	3	22	1	1	1							1	1	2				

1987-88

							Att.
1	Aug	15	(h)	Queen's Park R	L 0-3		22,881
2		22	(a)	Luton T	D 2-2	Brady, Stewart (pen)	8,073
3		29	(h)	Norwich C	W 2-0	Cottee 2	16,394
4		31	(a)	Portsmouth	L 1-2	Strodder	16,104
5	Sep	5	(h)	Liverpool	D 1-1	Cottee	29,865
6		12	(a)	Wimbledon	D 1-1	Cottee	8,507
7		19	(h)	Tottenham H	L 0-1		27,750
8		26	(a)	Arsenal	L 0-1		40,127
9	Oct	3	(h)	Derby Co	D 1-1	Brady	17,226
10		10	(h)	Charlton A	D 1-1	Ince	15,757
11		17	(a)	Oxford U	W 2-1	Cottee, Caton (og)	9,092
12		25	(h)	Manchester U	D 1-1	Stewart (pen)	19,863
13		31	(a)	Watford	W 2-1	Dickens, Cottee	14,427
14	Nov	7	(h)	Sheffield W	L 0-1		16,277
15		14	(a)	Everton	L 1-3	Hilton	29,405
16		21	(h)	Nottingham F	W 3-2	Cottee 2, Stewart (pen)	17,216
17		28	(a)	Coventry C	D 0-0		16,740
18	Dec	55	(h)	Southampton	W 2-1	Keen, Dickens	15,375
19		12	(a)	Chelsea	D 1-1	Parris	22,850
20		19	(h)	Newcastle U	W 2-1	Robson, Ince	18,679
21		26	(h)	Wimbledon	L 1-2	Stewart (pen)	18,605
22		28	(a)	Tottenham H	L 1-2	Hilton	39,456
23	Jan	1	(a)	Norwich C	L 1-4	Cottee	20,069
24		2	(h)	Luton T	D 1-1	Ince	16,716
25		16	(a)	Queen's Park R	W 1-0	Dickens	14,509
26	Feb	6	(a)	Liverpool	D 0-0		42,049
27		13	(h)	Portsmouth	D 1-1	Cottee	18,639
28		27	(a)	Derby Co	L 0-1		16,301
29	Mar	5	(h)	Oxford U	D 1-1	Ward	14,980
30		12	(a)	Charlton A	L 0-3		8,118
31		19	(h)	Watford	W 1-0	Rosenior	16,051
32		26	(a)	Manchester U	L 1-3	Rosenior	37,269
33	Apr	2	(a)	Sheffield W	L 1-2	Rosenior	18,435
34		4	(h)	Everton	D 0-0		21,195
35		12	(h)	Arsenal	L 0-1		26,746
36		20	(a)	Nottingham F	D 0-0		15,775
37		23	(h)	Coventry C	D 1-1	Cottee	17,733
38		30	(a)	Southampton	L 1-2	Cottee	15,652
39	May	2	(h)	Chelsea	W 4-1	Rosenior 2, Hilton, Cottee	28,521
40		7	(a)	Newcastle U	L 1-2	Robson	23,731

FINAL LEAGUE POSITION: 16th in Division One

Appearances

Sub. Appearances

Goals

46

McAlister	Stewart	McQueen	Orr	Martin	Devonshire	Ward	McAvennie	Brady	Cottee	Robson	Strodder	Dickens	Ince	Parris	Hilton	Keen	Slater	Dolan	Bonds	Gale	Potts	Rosenior	Dicks	Parkes	
1	2*	3	4	5	6†	7	8	9	10	11	12	14													1
1	2	3		5		7	8	6	10	11	4		9												2
1	2	3		5		7	8	6	10	11	4		9												3
1	2*	3		5		7	8	6	10	11	4		9	12											4
1	2	3*		5		7	8	6	10	11	4		9	12											5
1	2			5		7	8	6	10	11	4		9	3											6
1	2			5		7	8	6	10	11	4*		9	3	12										7
1	2			5			8	6	10	11	4		9	3		7									8
1	2†	3*		5				6	10	11	4		9	8	12	7	14								9
1	2			5		7		6	10	11		8	9	3		4									10
1	2			5		7		6	10	11		8	9	3		4									11
1	2	11		5		7		6	10			8	9	3		4									2
1	2			5		7		6	10	11		8	9	3		4									13
1	2			5		7		6	10	11		8	9	3		4*		12							14
1		5†				7		6	10	11	12	8	9	3*	4	14			2						15
1	5					7			10	11		8	9	3	4	6			2						16
1	5					7			10	11		8	9	3	4	6			2						17
1	5					7			10	11	4	8	9	3		6			2						18
1	5					7			10	11	4	8		3	9	6			2						19
1	5							7	10	11	4	8	9	3	12	6			2*						20
1	5					7		14	10	11	4	8†	9	3*	12	6			2						21
1	5					7*		8	10	11	12		9	3	4	6			2						22
1	5					7			10	11		8	9†	3	4	6*		12	2	14					23
1	5					7			10	11	4		12	3*	9				2	8	6				24
1	2	3				7		8	10	11	5	9							4	6					25
1	2	12				7		8	10	11	5	9*	3						4	6					26
1	2					7		8	10	11	5	9	3						4	6					27
1	2	12				7	8†		10	11	5	9*	3		14				4	6					28
1	2	3				7			10	11	5	9*			8			12	4	6					29
1	2	3				7			10	11	5	8*			12	9			4	6					30
1	2					7			10	11*	5	12			8				4	6	3	9			31
1	2					7			10		5	11		12	8*				4	6	3	9			32
1	2					7			10	11	5†	12	8					4*	6	14	9	3			33
1	2*					7			10	11	5	8	12	4						6		9	3		34
						7			10	11	5				8		12		4	6	2*	9	3	1	35
1						7			10	11	5	8			2					6		9	3		36
1						7			10	11	5	8	9*	2	12	4†	14		6				3		37
1						7			10		5	8		11					4	6	2	9	3		38
1						7			10	11		8		2	5					6	4	9	3		39
1						7			10	11		8		2	5					6	4	9	3		40
39	33	10	1	15	1	37	8	21	40	37	27	25	26	27	9	19	1	22	17	7	9	8	1		
	2							1			3	3	2	3	5	4	2	3		1	1				
	4						1	2	13	2	1	3	3	1	3	1						5			

1988-89

#	Month	Date		Opponent	Res	Score	Scorers	Att
1	Aug	27	(a)	Southampton	L	0-4		18,407
2	Sep	3	(h)	Charlton A	L	1-3	Keen (pen)	19,566
3		10	(a)	Wimbledon	W	1-0	Ward	7,730
4		17	(h)	Aston Villa	D	2-2	Kelly, Mountfield (og)	19,186
5		24	(a)	Manchester U	L	0-2		39,941
6	Oct	1	(h)	Arsenal	L	1-4	Dickens	27,658
7		8	(a)	Middlesbrough	L	0-1		19,608
8		15	(a)	Queen's Park R	L	1-2	Kelly	14,566
9		22	(h)	Newcastle U	W	2-0	Dickens, Stewart (pen)	17,765
10		29	(h)	Liverpool	L	0-2		30,188
11	Nov	5	(a)	Coventry C	D	1-1	Kelly	14,651
12		12	(h)	Nottingham F	D	3-3	Kelly 2, Rosenior	21,682
13		19	(a)	Luton T	L	1-4	Martin	9,308
14		26	(h)	Everton	L	0-1		22,176
15	Dec	3	(a)	Millwall	W	1-0	Ince	20,105
16		10	(h)	Sheffield W	D	0-0		16,676
17		17	(h)	Tottenham H	L	0-2		28,379
18		27	(a)	Norwich C	L	1-2	Stewart (pen)	17,491
19		31	(a)	Charlton A	D	0-0		11,084
20	Jan	2	(h)	Wimbledon	L	1-2	Rosenior	18,346
21		14	(a)	Derby Co	W	2-1	Brady, Kelly	16,796
22		21	(h)	Manchester U	L	1-3	Brady (pen)	29,822
23	Feb	4	(a)	Arsenal	L	1-2	Dicks	40,139
24		25	(h)	Queen's Park R	D	0-0		17,371
25	Mar	11	(h)	Coventry C	D	1-1	Ince	15,205
26		25	(a)	Aston Villa	W	1-0	Ince	22,471
27		27	(h)	Norwich C	L	0-2		27,265
28	Apr	1	(a)	Tottenham H	L	0-3		28,375
29		8	(h)	Derby Co	D	1-1	Rosenior	16,230
30		11	(h)	Middlesbrough	L	1-2	Keen	16,217
31		15	(h)	Southampton	L	1-2	Brady (pen)	14,766
32		22	(h)	Millwall	W	3-0	Dickens, Dicks, Parris	16,603
33	May	3	(a)	Newcastle U	W	2-1	Keen, Ward	14,202
34		6	(h)	Luton T	W	1-0	Dickens	18,686
35		9	(a)	Sheffield W	W	2-0	Dickens, Rosenior	19,905
36		13	(a)	Everton	L	1-3	Slater	21,694
37		18	(a)	Nottingham F	W	2-1	Rosenior 2	20,843
38		23	(a)	Liverpool	L	1-5	Rosenior	41,855

FINAL LEAGUE POSITION: 19th in Division One

Appearances

Sub. Appearances

Goals

Appearances and scoring grid (shirt numbers per match). `*` and `†` denote substitutions.

McAlister	Potts	Dicks	Gale	Martin	Keen	Ward	Parris	Slater	Kelly	Robson	Dickens	Hilton	Ince	Devonshire	McKnight	Rosenior	Strodder	Stewart	Brady	Parkes	McAvennie	McQueen	
1	2	3	4*	5	6	7	8	9†	10	11	14	12											1
1	2*	3		5	6†	7	8	9	10	11	4		12	14									2
		3		5		7	2		8*	11	10	4	6	12	1	9							3
		3		5		7	2		8	11	10		6	12	1	9	4*						4
		3				7	2		8	11	10	5	6	12	1	9	4*						5
		3		5		7	2†		8	11	10	4	6	12	1	9*	14						6
	2*	3	4		12	7	9		8		10	5	11	6	1								7
	2	3	4		12	7			8		10	5	11	6*	1	9							8
		3	4	5	12	7		9	8		10		11	6*	1			2					9
		3	4	5		7		9	8*		10		11	6	1	12		2					10
	2	3	4	5	6	7			8		10		11		1	9							11
	2	3	4	5	6	7	12		8†		10		11*		1	9			14				12
	2	3	4	5	6*	7	12				10†	14	11		1	9			8				13
	2	3	4	5	6	7*					10		11	12	1	9			8				14
	2	3	4	5					8		10		11	6	1	9			7				15
	2	4		5		3			8		10		11	6	1	9			7				16
	2	4		5	12	3			8		10		11	6*	1	9			7				17
	2	4		5*	14	3			8		10†		11	6	1	9		12	7				18
	11	3	4	5	6	12			8		10				1	9		2	7*				19
	11	3	4	5	6				8		10				1	9		2	7				20
	5	3	4	12					8		10		11	6	1	9	14	2†	7*				21
	2	3	4	5	12	10	8†						11	6*	1	9		14	7				22
	2	3	4		7			12	8				11	6*	1	9	5		10				23
	2	3	4	5		7	12	9	8*				11	6					10	1			24
	2	3	4	5				9	8		10		11	6					7	1			25
		3	4		7	2		9	12	5			11	6*					10	1	8		26
		3	4		7	2		9	10	5			11			12			6*	1	8		27
	6	3	4		7	2		9	12				11				5*		10	1	8		28
	14	3	4†	5		7	2	12			6		11			9			10*	1	8		29
	4	3		11	7	2			6	5						9			10	1	8		30
	4		3		7	2	12		6*	5			11			9			10†	1	8	14	31
	5	3	4	10	7	2	9		6				11*							1	8	12	32
		3	4	5	10	7	2	9	12		6		11							1	8*		33
	14	3	4†	5	10	7	2		8	12	6		11			9*				1			34
	12	3	4*	5	10	7	2		8		6		11			9				1			35
	12	3	4	5	10†	7	2	14	8		6		11*			9				1			36
	12	3	4	5	10	7	2		8		6				1	9			11*				37
		3	4	5	14	7	2		8		6		11†		1	9			10*	12			38
2	23	34	31	27	16	30	23	16	21	6	37	9	32	14	23	26	4	5	21	13	8		
	5			8		4	2	4		3	2	1	6		2	3	1	1		1	2		
	2		1	3	2	1	1	6		5		3			7		2	3					

1989-90

1	Aug	10	(a)	Stoke C	D	1-1	Keen	16,058
2		23	(h)	Bradford C	W	2-0	Slater 2	19,914
3		26	(h)	Plymouth A	W	3-2	Allen, Keen, Kelly	20,231
4	Sep	2	(a)	Hull C	D	1-1	Ward	9,235
5		9	(h)	Swindon T	D	1-1	Allen	21,469
6		16	(a)	Brighton & HA	L	0-3		12,689
7		23	(h)	Watford	W	1-0	Dicks (pen)	20,728
8		26	(a)	Portsmouth	W	1-0	Rosenior	12,632
9		30	(h)	West Brom A	L	2-3	Dolan, Parris	19,739
10	Oct	7	(h)	Leeds U	L	0-1		23,539
11		14	(a)	Sheffield U	W	2-0	Ward 2 (1 pen)	20,822
12		18	(h)	Sunderland	W	5-0	Dolan 2, Allen, Keen, Slater	20,901
13		21	(a)	Port Vale	D	2-2	Keen, Slater	8,899
14		28	(h)	Oxford U	W	3-2	Dicks, Parris, Slater	19,177
15	Nov	1	(a)	Bournemouth	D	1-1	Strodder	9,979
16		4	(a)	Wolverhampton W	L	0-1		22,231
17		11	(h)	Newcastle U	D	0-0		25,892
18		18	(h)	Middlesbrough	W	2-0	Dicks (pen), Slater	18,720
19		25	(a)	Blackburn R	L	4-5	Brady, Dicks (pen), Slater, Ward	10,215
20	Dec	2	(h)	Stoke C	D	0-0		17,704
21		9	(a)	Bradford C	L	1-2	Ward	9,257
22		16	(h)	Oldham A	L	0-2		14,960
23		26	(a)	Ipswich T	L	0-1		24,365
24		30	(a)	Leicester C	L	0-1		16,925
25	Jan	1	(h)	Barnsley	W	4-2	Keen 2, Allen, Dicks (pen)	18,391
26		13	(a)	Plymouth A	D	1-1	Quinn	11,671
27		20	(h)	Hull C	L	1-2	Morley	16,847
28	Feb	10	(h)	Brighton & HA	W	3-1	Gatting (og), Dicks, Quinn	19,101
29		18	(a)	Swindon T	D	2-2	Quinn 2	16,105
30		24	(h)	Blackburn R	D	1-1	Quinn	20,052
31	Mar	3	(a)	Middlesbrough	W	1-0	Allen	23,617
32		10	(h)	Portsmouth	W	2-1	Allen, Dicks (pen)	20,961
33		13	(a)	Watford	W	1-0	Morley	15,682
34		17	(a)	Leeds U	L	2-3	Morley, Foster	32,536
35		21	(h)	Sheffield U	W	5-0	Quinn 3 (1 pen), Allen, Morley	21,629
36		24	(a)	Sunderland	L	3-4	Quinn 2, Morley	13,896
37		31	(h)	Port Vale	D	2-2	Gale, Morley	20,507
38	Apr	4	(a)	West Brom A	W	3-1	Bishop, Keen, Quinn	11,556
39		7	(a)	Oxford U	W	2-0	Morley, Quinn	8,371
40		11	(h)	Bournemouth	W	4-1	Allen, Bishop, Dicks (pen), Miller (og)	20,202
41		14	(a)	Barnsley	D	1-1	Morley	10,344
42		17	(h)	Ipswich T	W	2-0	Allen, Keen	25,178
43		21	(a)	Oldham A	L	0-3		12,190
44		28	(a)	Newcastle U	L	1-2	Dicks (pen)	31,496
45	May	2	(h)	Leicester C	W	3-1	Keen, Morley, Rosenior	17,939
46		5	(h)	Wolverhampton W	W	4-0	Brady, Keen, Morley, Robson	22,509

FINAL LEAGUE POSITION: 7th in Division Two

Appearances

Sub. Appearances

Goals

Parkes	Potts	Parris	Gale	Martin	Keen	Ward	McAvennie	Slater	Brady	Ince	Kelly D	Dicks	Allen	Devonshire	Dolan	Foster	Rosenior	Strodder	Fashanu	McQueen	Suckling	Bishop	Morley	Quinn	Kelly P	Robson	Miklosko	#
1	2	3	4	5	6	7	8*	9	10	11	12																	1
1	2	11	4	5	6	7		9	10		8	3																2
1	2	11	4	5	6	7			10		8	3	9															3
1	2		4	5	6	7		11	10*		8	3	9	12														4
1	2	11	4	5	6	7			10*		8†	3	9	12	14													5
1	2	11	4	5	6	7		8	10			3	9															6
1	2	11	4	5	6			8				3	7		9*	10	12											7
1	2	11	4	5	6			8				3	7			10	9											8
1	2	11	4	5	6			8	9*			3	7		12	10												9
1	2	11	4*	5	6	7		8	12			3	9			10												10
1	2	11		5	6	7		8				3	9			10		4										11
1	2	11		5	6	7		8	12			3*	10			9		4										12
1	2	11		5	6	7		8				3	10			9		4										13
1	2	11		5	6			8	7			3	10			9		4										14
1	2	11		5	6*	12		8	7			3	10			9		4										15
1	2	11		5	6*	12		8†	7			3	10			9	14	4										16
1	2	11		5	6	10		8	7*		14	3			12	9†		4										17
1	2	11		5	6	10		8	7			3	9		4													18
1	2			5		10		8	7			3	9	6	4			11										19
1	2			5	9	10		8	7		12	3		6*	14			4	11†									20
1	2	6		5	9	10		8	7				11			4		3										21
	2	6		5	14	10		8	7			3	11	12		9*	4†			1								22
	2	12	6	5	9	10		8†	7*		14	3	11				4			✓								23
	2	11	6	5				10				3	7				4				1	8	9					24
	2	4	6	5	9*							12	3	11							1	8	10	7				25
	2	14	6	5	9†				12			3	7	6*							1	8	10	11				26
	2†		6	5	11				7		12					4*		3		1		8	10	9	14			27
1		4*	6	5	11			10	7		9	3										8		12	2			28
		4	6	5	11†			10*	7		14	3	8										12	9	2	1		29
		4	6	5	11			10	7*		14	3	8										12	9	2†	1		30
		4	6	5	11			10	7*			3	8										12	14	9†	2	1	31
		4	6		10			2	7†		11	3	8		5	9*							12				1	32
		4	6		10			2				3	8		5							7	11	9			1	33
		4*	6		10			2	12				8		5			3				7	11	9			1	34
		4	6		10			2					8		5			3				7	11	9			1	35
		4	6		10*			2	12				8		5							7	11	9			1	36
		4	6		10*	14		2	7†			3	8		5								7	11	9†		1	37
		4	6		10			2				3	8		5								7	11	9		1	38
		4	6		10*			2				3	8		5			12				7	11	9			1	39
	12	4*	6		10			14	2			3	8		5							7	11†	9			1	40
		4	6		7			2	11			3	8		5								10	9			1	41
	12	4	6		10	14		2	7*			3	8		5								11†	9			1	42
		4	6		10			2	7			3	8		5			12					11*	9			1	43
	4	12	6		10	14		2				3	8		5								11*	9†		7	1	44
	4		6		10*			2	12			3	8		5	9							11			7	1	45
	4		6		10*			2	12			3	8		5	9							11†	14		7	1	46
22	30	35	36	31	43	17	1	40	25	1	8	40	39	3	8	20	4	16	2	5	6	13	18	18		7	18	
	2	3			1	2	4		8		8			4	2	2	1			2		4	1	3	1			
		2	1		10	5		7	2		1	9	9		3			2	1			2	10	13		1		

1990-91

1	Aug	25	(a)	Middlesbrough	D	0-0		20,680
2		29	(h)	Portsmouth	D	1-1	McAvennie	20,835
3	Sep	1	(h)	Watford	W	1-0	Dicks (pen)	19,872
4		8	(a)	Leicester C	W	2-1	Morley, James (og)	14,605
5		15	(h)	Wolverhampton W	D	1-1	Martin	23,241
6		19	(h)	Ipswich T	W	3-1	Bishop, Morley, Quinn	18,764
7		22	(a)	Newcastle U	D	1-1	Morley	25,462
8		29	(a)	Sheffield W	D	1-1	Dicks	28,786
9	Oct	3	(h)	Oxford U	W	2-0	Foster, Morley	18,125
10		6	(h)	Hull C	W	7-1	Dicks 2 (1 pen), Quinn 2, Morley, Parris, Potts	19,472
11		13	(a)	Bristol C	D	1-1	McAvennie	16,838
12		20	(a)	Swindon T	W	1-0	McAvennie	13,658
13		24	(h)	Blackburn R	W	1-0	Bishop	20,003
14		27	(h)	Charlton A	W	2-1	Allen 2	24,019
15	Nov	3	(a)	Notts Co	W	1-0	Morley	10,781
16		10	(a)	Millwall	D	1-1	McAvennie	20,591
17		17	(h)	Brighton & HA	W	2-1	Foster, Slater	23,082
18		24	(a)	Plymouth A	W	1-0	McAvennie	11,490
19	Dec	1	(h)	West Brom A	W	3-1	McAvennie, Morley, Parris	24,753
20		8	(a)	Portsmouth	W	1-0	Morley	12,045
21		15	(h)	Middlesbrough	D	0-0		23,705
22		22	(a)	Barnsley	L	0-1		10,348
23		26	(h)	Oldham A	W	2-0	Morley, Slater	24,950
24		29	(h)	Port Vale	D	0-0		23,403
25	Jan	1	(a)	Bristol R	W	1-0	Quinn	7,932
26		12	(a)	Watford	W	1-0	Morley	17,172
27		19	(h)	Leicester C	W	1-0	Parris	21,652
28	Feb	2	(a)	Wolverhampton W	L	1-2	McAvennie	19,454
29		24	(h)	Millwall	W	3-1	McAvennie 2, Morley	20,503
30	Mar	2	(a)	West Brom A	D	0-0		16,089
31		5	(h)	Plymouth A	D	2-2	Breacker, Marker (og)	18,933
32		13	(a)	Oxford U	L	1-2	Quinn	8,225
33		16	(h)	Sheffield W	L	1-3	Quinn	26,182
34		20	(h)	Bristol C	W	1-0	Gale	22,951
35		23	(a)	Hull C	D	0-0		9,558
36		29	(a)	Oldham A	D	1-1	Bishop (pen)	16,932
37	Apr	1	(h)	Barnsley	W	3-2	Dowie, Foster, McAvennie	24,607
38		6	(a)	Port Vale	W	1-0	Bishop	9,658
39		10	(a)	Brighton & HA	L	0-1		11,904
40		17	(a)	Ipswich T	W	1-0	Morley	20,290
41		20	(h)	Swindon T	W	2-0	Dowie, Parris	25,944
42		24	(h)	Newcastle U	D	1-1	Dowie	24,195
43		27	(a)	Blackburn R	L	1-3	Dowie	10,808
44	May	4	(a)	Charlton A	D	1-1	Allen	16,137
45		8	(h)	Bristol R	W	1-0	Slater	23,054
46		11	(h)	Notts Co	L	1-2	Parris	26,551

FINAL LEAGUE POSITION: 2nd in Division Two

Appearances

Sub. Appearances

Goals

Miklosko	Potts	Dicks	Foster	Martin	Keen	Bishop	McAvennie	Slater	Allen	Morley	Quinn	Parris	Livett	Rush	Gale	Breacker	Hughton	Clarke	Robson	Carr	Rosenior	Dowie	Stewart	
1	2	3	4	5	6	7	8	9	10	11														1
1	2	3	4	5	6	7	8	9	10	11														2
1	2	3	4	5	6	7	8	9	10†	11*	12	14												3
1	2	3	4	5	6	7	8*	9†	10	11	12	14												4
1	2	3	4	5	6	7	8		10	11		12	9*											5
1	2†	3	4	5	6	7	8*	9	10	11	12	14												6
1	2	3	4	5	6	7	12	9†	10	11	8*	14												7
1	2	3	4	5†	6	7	12	9	10	11	8*	14												8
1	2	3	4	5	6	7		9*	10	11	8	12												9
1	2	3	4	5	6*	7	12		10	11	8†	9	14											10
1	2	3	4	5		7	12	9*	10	11	8	6												11
1	2	3†	4	5		7	12		10	11	8*	6			9	14								12
1		3†	4	5		7	12	14	10	11	8*	6			9	2								13
1			4	5	3	7	8	9*	10	11		6	12			2								14
1			4	5	8	7			10	11		3			9	2	6							15
1			4	5	8	7	9	10*		11		3			12	2	6							16
1			4	5	10	7	8	12		11		3			9*	2	6							17
1			4	5	10	7	8	9		11		3				2	6							18
1			4	5	10*	7	8	9	12	11		3				2	6							19
1		4	5†		7	8*	9	10	11	12		3			14	2	6							20
1	5				7	8	9	10	11*	12		3			4	2	6							21
1	5				7	8*	9	10	11	12		3			4	2	6							22
1		5				7	9	10	11	8		3			4	2	6							23
1	12	5				7	9	10*	11	8		3			4	2	6							24
1	8	5				7		10	11	9		3			4	2	6							25
1	10	5†			7	8		11	9*			3			4	2	6	12	14					26
1	10		7	5	12	8		11	9*			3			4	2	6							27
1	10		7	5	8	9*	14	11	12	3†					4	2	6							28
1	10		7	5	8	9	12	11		3					4*	2	6							29
1	10		7*	5	8	9	12	11		3					4	2	6							30
1	10	4	7	5	8	9	12		11	3						2	6*							31
1	10	5	14	7	8	12		11	3			4			2*	6			9†					32
1	2	5	10	7	8	9	12	11†	3			4				6*			14					33
1	2	5	10	7	8	9*	12	11†	3			4				6				14				34
1	2	5	10†	7	8*		11	3				4				6			14	12		9		35
1	2	5		7	8	10	11	3				4				6						9		36
1	2	5	12	7	8	10	11	3				4				6*						9		37
1	2	5	10	7		8	11	3				4				6						9		38
1	2	5	8	7		11	14	10	12	3						6†					9*	4		39
1	2	5†	10	7	12	8	14	11	3			4				6						9*		40
1	2		10*	7		8	12	11	3			4				6						9	5	41
1	2		10	7		8	12	11	3			4				6						9	5*	42
1	2		8	7		10*	12	11†	14	3					4	6						9	5	43
1	2			7		10	8	11	12	3					4	6						9*	5	44
1	4	5	14	7	12	8	10†	11	3						2	6						9*		45
1	2	5	14	7	12	8	10	11	3			4				6†						9*		46
46	36	13	36	20	36	40	24	37	28	38	16	37	1	2	23	23	32			1		12	5	
	1			4			10	3	12		10	7		3	1	1		1	1	2	2			
	1	4	3	1		4	10	3	3	12	6	5			1	1						4		

53

1991-92

1	Aug	17	(h)	Luton T	D	0-0		25,079
2		21	(a)	Sheffield U	D	1-1	Small	21,463
3		24	(a)	Wimbledon	L	0-2		10,081
4		28	(h)	Aston Villa	W	3-1	Small, Rosenior, Brown	23,644
5		31	(h)	Notts Co	L	0-2		20,093
6	Sep	4	(a)	Queen's Park R	D	0-0		16,616
7		7	(h)	Chelsea	D	1-1	Small	18,875
8		14	(a)	Norwich C	L	1-2	Small	15,348
9		17	(a)	Crystal Palace	W	3-2	Thomas, Morley, Small	21,363
10		21	(h)	Manchester C	L	1-2	Brown	25,558
11		28	(a)	Nottingham F	D	2-2	Small 2 (1 pen)	25,613
12	Oct	5	(h)	Coventry C	L	0-1		21,817
13		18	(a)	Oldham A	D	2-2	Small, McAvennie	14,365
14		26	(h)	Tottenham H	W	2-1	Small, Thomas	23,946
15	Nov	2	(a)	Arsenal	W	1-0	Small	33,539
16		17	(h)	Liverpool	D	0-0		23,569
17		23	(a)	Manchester U	L	1-2	McAvennie	47,185
18		30	(h)	Sheffield W	L	1-2	Breacker	24,116
19	Dec	7	(a)	Everton	L	0-4		21,563
20		21	(h)	Sheffield U	D	1-1	Dicks (pen)	19,287
21		26	(a)	Aston Villa	L	1-3	McAvennie	31,959
22		28	(a)	Notts Co	L	0-3		11,163
23	Jan	1	(h)	Leeds U	L	1-3	Dicks (pen)	21,766
24		11	(h)	Wimbledon	D	1-1	Morley	18,485
25		18	(a)	Luton T	W	1-0	Small	11,088
26	Feb	1	(h)	Oldham A	W	1-0	Thomas	19,012
27		22	(a)	Sheffield W	L	1-2	Small	26,150
28		29	(h)	Everton	L	0-2		20,976
29	Mar	3	(a)	Southampton	L	0-1		14,548
30		11	(a)	Liverpool	L	0-1		30,821
31		14	(h)	Arsenal	L	0-2		22,640
32		21	(h)	Queen's Park R	D	2-2	Small, Breacker	20,401
33		28	(a)	Leeds U	D	0-0		31,101
34	Apr	1	(a)	Tottenham H	L	0-3		31,809
35		4	(a)	Chelsea	L	1-2	Allen C	20,684
36		11	(h)	Norwich C	W	4-0	Rush 2, Dicks (pen), Bishop	16,896
37		14	(h)	Southampton	L	0-1		18,298
38		18	(a)	Manchester C	L	0-2		25,601
39		20	(h)	Crystal Palace	L	0-2		17,710
40		22	(h)	Manchester U	W	1-0	Brown	24,197
41		25	(a)	Coventry C	L	0-1		15,392
42	May	2	(h)	Nottingham F	W	3-0	McAvennie 3	20,629

FINAL LEAGUE POSITION: 22nd in Division One

Appearances

Sub. Appearances

Goals

Miklosko	Brown	Thomas	Breacker	Foster	Paris	Bishop	Slater	Small	Rosenior	Allen M	Keen	Morley	Rush	Parks	Hughton	Potts	Gale	McAvennie	Dicks	Atteveld	Allen C	Martin A	Clarke	Martin D	#
1	2	3	4	5	6	7*	8	9	10	11	12														1
1	2	3	4	5	6	7	8	9	10†	11*	12	14													2
1	2	3	4	5	6	7	8*	9	10	11†		14	12												3
1	2	3	4	5	6	7	8	9	10	11*	12														4
	2	3	4	5	6	7	8	9	10*	11†	12			1		14									5
	2	3	4	5	6	7	8	9†		11*	12	14		1		10									6
1	2	3	4	5	6	7	8	9		11						10									7
1	2	3	4	5	6†	7	8	9		11*	12	14				10									8
1	2	3	4	5	6	7	8	9		11						10									9
1	2	3	4	5	6	7	8	9		11*	12					10									10
1		3	2	5	6	7	8	9*		11	12					10	4								11
1	5	3†	2		6	7	8	9		11*	12	14				10	4								12
1		3	2		6	7	8†	9		11*	10	14				5	4	12							13
1		3	2		6	7	11	9			12	10*				5	4	8							14
1		3	2		6	7	11	9				10				5	4	8							15
1		3	2		6	7	11	9				10				5	4	8							16
1		3	2		6	7	11	9			12	10*				5	4	8							17
1		3	2		6	7	11	9			12	10*				5	4	8							18
1		3	2		6*	7	11	9			12	10				5	4	8							19
1	2				6	7	11	9*			12	10				5	4	8	3						20
1			2		6	7	11	9*			12	10				5	4	8	3						21
1			2	6		7	11	9				10				5	4	8	3						22
1		6	2			7	11	9*			12	10				5	4	8	3						23
1	9	6*	2	5		7	11	14	10†		12						4	8	3						24
1	9	6	2	5		7	11*	14			12	10					4	8†	3						25
	9	6	2	5		7	11	12				10*		1			4	8	3						26
	12		2	5		7	11	9			8*	10		1			4		3	6					27
	8	6	2†	5		7	11*	9			12	10	14	1			4		3						28
	8	6†		5		7	11	9			12	10	14	1		2	4*		3						29
1	2	6*				7	11	9			8	10	12			5	4		3						30
1	2			5	14	7	11	9			6	10†	12				4	8*	3						31
1	2	12	14	5		7*	11	9			6†	10					4	8	3						32
1	2	8	4	5		7	11*	9			6	10†				14		12	3						33
1	2†	8	6*	5		7	11	9			10	14				4		12	3						34
1	2	9		5		7	11*				6	12				4		8	3		10				35
1	6	2				7	11	9*			8	12					4		3		10	5			36
1	2					7	11	9			6	12				8*	4		3		10	5			37
1	2					7	11	9*			6	10					4	8	3			5	12		38
1	12	6	2*			7	11	9			8						4		3		10	5			39
1	10	6				7	11	9			8					2	4		3			5			40
1	10†	6				7*	11	9			8	12				2	4		3			5	14		41
1		6				7	11	9			8					2	4	12	3			5		10	42
36	25	34	33	24	20	41	41	37	5	14	20	13	3	6		34	24	16	23	1	4	7		1	
2	1	1		1		3	4	5	9	11	7		1			1	4					1	1		
3	3	2			1		13	1		2	2					6	3		1						

1992-93

1	Aug	16	(a)	Barnsley	W	1-0	Allen C	6,791
2		22	(h)	Charlton A	L	0-1		17,054
3		29	(a)	Newcastle U	L	0-2		29,855
4	Sep	5	(h)	Watford	W	2-1	Allen C, Allen M	11,921
5		12	(a)	Peterborough U	W	3-1	Allen M, Morley, Keen	10,657
6		15	(a)	Bristol C	W	5-1	Robson, Morley 2, Allen C 2	14,130
7		20	(h)	Derby Co	D	1-1	Morley	11,493
8		27	(a)	Portsmouth	W	1-0	Allen C	12,158
9	Oct	4	(a)	Wolverhampton W	D	0-0		14,391
10		11	(h)	Sunderland	W	6-0	Martin, Morley, Allen M, Robson 2, Keen	10,326
11		17	(a)	Bristol R	W	4-0	Dicks (pen), Morley, Allen C, Keen	6,189
12		24	(h)	Swindon T	L	0-1		17,842
13		31	(a)	Cambridge U	L	1-2	Morley	7,214
14	Nov	3	(a)	Grimsby T	D	1-1	Morley	9,119
15		7	(h)	Notts Co	W	2-0	Allen C, Morley	12,345
16		15	(a)	Millwall	L	1-2	Robson	12,445
17		21	(h)	Oxford U	W	5-3	Allen C, Breacker, Dicks 2, Morley	11,842
18		28	(h)	Birmingham C	W	3-1	Allen C 2, Morley	15,004
19	Dec	4	(a)	Tranmere R	L	2-5	Allen C, Morley	11,782
20		12	(h)	Southend U	W	2-0	Allen C, Morley	15,739
21		20	(a)	Brentford	D	0-0		11,912
22		26	(a)	Charlton A	D	1-1	Dicks	8,337
23		28	(h)	Luton T	D	2-2	Dicks (pen), Breacker	18,786
24	Jan	10	(a)	Derby Co	W	2-0	Robson, Morley	13,737
25		16	(h)	Portsmouth	W	2-0	Morley, Foster	18,127
26		27	(h)	Bristol C	W	2-0	Morley, Robson	12,118
27		30	(a)	Leicester C	W	2-1	Robson, Gale	18,838
28	Feb	6	(h)	Barnsley	D	1-1	Jones	14,101
29		9	(h)	Peterborough U	W	2-1	Butler, Jones	12,537
30		13	(a)	Watford	W	2-1	Robson, Keen	13,115
31		21	.(h)	Newcastle U	D	0-0		24,159
32		27	(a)	Sunderland	D	0-0		19,068
33	Mar	6	(h)	Wolverhampton W	W	3-1	Morley, Dicks (pen), Mountfield (og)	24,679
34		9	(h)	Grimsby T	W	2-1	Dicks 2	13,170
35		13	(a)	Notts Co	L	0-1		10,272
36		20	(h)	Tranmere R	W	2-0	Dicks 2 (2 pens)	16,369
37		23	(a)	Oxford U	L	0-1		9,506
38		28	(h)	Millwall	D	2-2	Keen, Morley	15,723
39	Apr	3	(a)	Birmingham C	W	2-1	Brown, Bishop	19,053
40		7	(a)	Southend U	L	0-1		12,813
41		11	(h)	Leicester C	W	3-0	Speedie 2, Keen	13,951
42		13	(a)	Luton T	L	0-2		10,959
43		17	(h)	Brentford	W	4-0	Butler, Keen, Morley, Allen M	16,522
44		24	(h)	Bristol R	W	2-1	Dicks (pen), Speedie	16,682
45	May	2	(a)	Swindon T	W	3-1	Morley, Allen C, Brown	17,004
46		8	(h)	Cambridge U	W	2-0	Speedie, Allen C	27,399

FINAL LEAGUE POSITION: 2nd in Division One

Appearances

Sub. Appearances

Goals

56

Miklosko	Breacker	Dicks	Potts	Martin	Parris	Bishop	Butler	Small	Allen C	Keen	Robson	Gale	Holmes	Allen M	Morley	Thomas	Brown	Clarke	Foster	Bunberry	Jones	Speedie	
1	2	3	4	5	6*	7	8	9	10*	11	12	14											1
1	2	3	4	5	6	7*	8	9	10	11	12												2
1	2	3	4	5		7	8	12	10	11				6*	9								3
1	2	3	4	5	12		8		10	11	7*			6	9								4
1	2		4	5			8	12	10*	11	7			6	9	3							5
1	2		4	5			8	12	10	11	7*			6	9	3							6
1	2		4	5			8	12	10	11	7*			6	9	3							7
1	2	3	4	5			8		10	11	7*		12	6	9								8
1	2	3	4	5			8		10†	11	7*	14	12	6	9								9
1	2	3	4	5			8		10	11	7			6	9								10
1	2	3	4	5			8		10	11	7			6	9								11
1	2		4	5	3		8		10	11	7			6	9								12
1	2		4	5	3		8		10	11	7			6	9								13
1	2		4	5	3		8		10	11	7*		12	6	9								14
1	2		4	5			8		10	11	7			6	9		3						15
1	2		4	5	6				10	11*	7			8	9		3	12					16
1	2	3	4	5	6				10	11*	7			8	9			12					17
1	2	3	4		6		12		10	11*	7	5		8	9								18
1	2	3	4	5	6*		12		10	11	7	14		8†	9								19
1	2	3	4	5	6*		12		10	11	7			8	9								20
1	2	3	4	5			8		10	11	7*			6	9				12				21
1	2	3	4	5	6*				10	11	7			8	9				12				22
1	2	3	4	5			8		10	11	7			6	9				⁄				23
1	2	3	4	5	12		8		10	11	7*			6	9		14						24
1	2	3	4		12		8		10*	11	7†	14		6	9		5						25
1	2		4		12		8			11	7†	5	14	6	9		3		10*				26
1	2		4		12		8			11†	7*	5	10	6	9		3			14			27
1	2	3	4				8			11	7	5		6	9					10			28
1	2	3	4				8			11*	7	5	12	6	9					10			29
1	2	3	4		14		8			11	7*	5	12	6	9					10†			30
1		3	4		10		8			11*	7	5		6	9		2			12			31
1		3	4		14	6	8			11	7†	5	12		9		2		10*				32
1		3	4		6		8		10	11*	7	5	12		9		2						33
1		3	4		12		8		10*	11	7	5		6	9		2						34
1		3	4		12		8		10	11	7*	5		6	9		2						35
1		3	4				8			11	7*	5	12	6	10		2				9		36
1		3	4				8			11*	12	5	7	6	10		2				9		37
1	2		4		6		8			11	7	5			10		3				9		38
1	2		4		6		8			11	7*	5	12	14	10†		3				9		39
1	2	3	4		6		8			11	7	5			10						9		40
1	2	3	4		6		8			11	7	5			10						9		41
1	2	3	4		6		8			11		5	12	7*	10						9		42
1	2	3	4				8			11	7	5		6	10						9		43
1	2	3	4		12		8			11	7*	5		6	10						9		44
1	2	3	4		6		8			11	7*	5		14	10†						9		45
1	2	3	4		6	12	8			11	7*	5		14	10						9†		46
46	39	34	46	23	10	15	39	5	25	46	41	21	6	33	41	3	13	3	2	4	11		
					6	7		4	2			3	2	12	1		2	1	3	2	2		
	2	11		1	1	2			14	7	8	1	1	4	20		2		1		2	4	

1993-94

1	Aug	14	(h)	Wimbledon	L	0-2		20,369
2		17	(a)	Leeds U	L	0-1		34,588
3		21	(a)	Coventry C	D	1-1	Gordon	12,864
4		25	(h)	Sheffield W	W	2-0	Allen C 2	19,441
5		28	(h)	Queen's Park R	L	0-4		18,084
6	Sep	1	(a)	Manchester U	L	0-3		44,613
7		11	(h)	Swindon T	D	0-0		15,777
8		18	(a)	Blackburn R	W	2-0	Chapman, Morley	14,437
9		25	(a)	Newcastle U	L	0-2		34,179
10	Oct	2	(h)	Chelsea	W	1-0	Morley	18,917
11		16	(h)	Aston Villa	D	0-0		20,416
12		23	(a)	Norwich C	D	0-0		20,175
13	Nov	1	(h)	Manchester C	W	3-1	Burrows, Chapman, Holmes	16,605
14		6	(a)	Liverpool	L	0-2		42,254
15		20	(h)	Oldham A	W	2-0	Martin, Morley	17,211
16		24	(h)	Arsenal	D	0-0		20,279
17		29	(a)	Southampton	W	2-0	Morley, Chapman	13,258
18	Dec	4	(a)	Wimbledon	W	2-1	Chapman 2	10,903
19		8	(h)	Leeds U	L	0-1		20,468
20		11	(h)	Coventry C	W	3-2	Breacker, Butler, Morley (pen)	17,243
21		18	(a)	Sheffield W	L	0-5		26,350
22		27	(a)	Ipswich T	D	1-1	Chapman	20,988
23		28	(h)	Tottenham H	L	1-3	Holmes	20,787
24	Jan	1	(a)	Everton	W	1-0	Breacker	19,602
25		3	(h)	Sheffield U	D	0-0		20,365
26		15	(a)	Aston Villa	L	1-3	Allen M	28,869
27		24	(h)	Norwich C	D	3-3	Sutton (og), Jones, Morley	20,738
28	Feb	12	(a)	Manchester C	D	0-0		29,118
29		25	(h)	Manchester U	D	2-2	Chapman, Morley	28,832
30	Mar	5	(a)	Swindon T	D	1-1	Morley	15,929
31		19	(h)	Newcastle U	L	2-4	Breacker, Martin	23,132
32		26	(a)	Chelsea	L	0-2		19,545
33		28	(a)	Sheffield U	L	2-3	Bishop, Holmes	13,646
34	Apr	2	(h)	Ipswich T	W	2-1	Rush, Morley	18,307
35		4	(a)	Tottenham H	W	4-1	Jones, Morley 2 (1 pen), Marsh	31,502
36		9	(h)	Everton	L	0-1		20,243
37		16	(a)	Oldham A	W	2-1	Allen M, Morley	11,669
38		23	(h)	Liverpool	L	1-2	Allen M	26,106
39		27	(h)	Blackburn R	L	1-2	Allen M	22,186
40		30	(a)	Arsenal	W	2-0	Morley, Allen M	33,700
41	May	3	(a)	Queen's Park R	D	0-0		10,350
42		7	(h)	Southampton	D	3-3	Williamson, Allen M, Monkou (og)	26,952

FINAL LEAGUE POSITION: 13th in F.A. Premier League

Appearances

Sub. Appearances

Goals

Miklosko	Breacker	Dicks	Potts	Gale	Allen M	Gordon	Butler	Morley	Allen C	Holmes	Rowland	Foster	Robson	Bishop	Jones	Rush	Burrows	Chapman	Marsh	Brown	Boere	Martin	Marquis	Mitchell	Williamson	
1	2	3	4	5	6	7	8	9	10	11*	12															1
1	2	3	4†	6	11	7	8	9	10*		12	5	14													2
1	2	3	4		6	7	8	9	10		11	5														3
1	2	3	4		6	7*	8	9	10	12	11	5														4
1	2	3	4		6		8	9	10		11	5	7													5
1	2	3	4	12	6*	7†		9	10	8	11	5	14													6
1	2	3	4	5		7*		9		8	11			6	10	12										7
1			4	5	12	7		11		8	2			6			3	9	10*							8
1			4	5	12	7		8†		11				6			3	9	10	2*	14					9
1	2		4	5	12		7	8		11				6			3	9	10*							10
1	2		4	5			7	8		11				6			3	9	10							11
1	2		4	5*			7	8		11	12			6			3	9	10							12
1	2		4				7	8		11*	12			6			3	9	10			5				13
1	2		4				7	8		11				6			3	9	10			5				14
1	2		4				7	8		11				6			3	9	10			5				15
1	2		4	5			7	8		11				6			3	9	10							16
1	2		4	5	10		7	8		11				6			3	9								17
1	2		4	5	10		7	8		11				6			3	9								18
1	2		4	5			7	8*		11				6			3	9	10		12					19
1	2		4	5	12		7	8		11				6*			3	9	10							20
1	2		4	5	12		7	8		11†				6*			3	9	10		14					21
1	2		4	5			7	8		11*	12			6			3	9	10		✓					22
1	2		4	5			7	8		11*				6	12		3	9	10							23
1	2		4	5			7	8		11*	12			6			3	9	10							24
1	2		4	5			7	8*		11				6	12		3	9	10							25
1	2		4	5	7			8*		11	3			6	12			9	10							26
1	2		4	5†	7			12		11	3			6	8			9*	10	14						27
1	2		4		7			12	10*	11	3			6				9	8†	5			14			28
1	2		4		7			8		11				6			3	9	10			5				29
1	2		4		7			8		11*	12			6			3	9	10			5				30
1	2		4				7	8*		11	3			6				9	10	12		5				31
1	2		4	5	7†		8	12		11				6	14		3†	9	10							32
1	2		4	5	12		7	8		11*	3			6				9	10†	14						33
1	2		4	5			7	9		11	3			6	8*				10	12						34
1	2		4	5			7*	9		11	3			6	12	8			10							35
1	2		4	5				9		11	3*			6	7	8			10		12					36
1	2			5	7			9		11				6		8	3		10	4						37
1	2		4	5	7			9		11				6*		8	3	12	10							38
1	2		4	5	7			9		11†				6	8*			12	10	3			14			39
1	2		4	5	7			9						6		8	3*		10	11				12		40
1	2		4	5	7			9						6		8*		12	10	3					11	41
1	2		4	5	7			9						6*		8	3	12	10						11	42
42	40	7	41	31	20	8	26	39	7	33	16	5	1	36	3	9	25	26	33	6		6			2	
			1	6				3		1	7		2		5	1		4		3	4	1	1	1	1	
	3				6	1	1	13	2	3				1	2	1	1	7	1			2			1	

59

1994-95

#	Month	Date		Opponent	Result		Scorers	Attendance
1	Aug	20	(h)	Leeds U	D	0-0		18,610
2		24	(a)	Manchester C	L	0-3		19,150
3		27	(a)	Norwich C	L	0-1		19,110
4		31	(h)	Newcastle U	L	1-3	Hutchison (pen)	17,375
5	Sep	10	(a)	Liverpool	D	0-0		30,907
6		17	(h)	Aston Villa	W	1-0	Cottee	18,326
7		25	(h)	Arsenal	L	0-2		18,495
8	Oct	2	(a)	Chelsea	W	2-1	Allen, Moncur	18,696
9		8	(h)	Crystal Palace	W	1-0	Hutchison	16,959
10		15	(a)	Manchester U	L	0-1		43,795
11		22	(h)	Southampton	W	2-0	Allen, Rush	18,853
12		29	(a)	Tottenham H	L	1-3	Rush	26,271
13	Nov	1	(a)	Everton	L	0-1		28,353
14		5	(h)	Leicester C	W	1-0	Dicks (pen)	18,780
15		19	(a)	Sheffield W	L	0-1		25,300
16		26	(h)	Coventry C	L	0-1		17,251
17	Dec	4	(a)	Queen's Park R	L	1-2	Boere	12,780
18		10	(a)	Leeds U	D	2-2	Boere 2	28,987
19		17	(h)	Manchester C	W	3-0	Cottee 3	17,286
20		26	(h)	Ipswich T	D	1-1	Cottee	20,562
21		28	(a)	Wimbledon	L	0-1		11,212
22		31	(h)	Nottingham F	W	3-1	Cottee, Bishop, Hughes	20,644
23	Jan	2	(a)	Blackburn R	L	2-4	Cottee, Dicks	25,503
24		14	(h)	Tottenham H	L	1-2	Boere	24,578
25		23	(h)	Sheffield W	L	0-2		14,554
26	Feb	4	(a)	Leicester C	W	2-1	Cottee, Dicks (pen)	20,375
27		13	(h)	Everton	D	2-2	Cottee 2	21,081
28		18	(a)	Coventry C	L	0-2		17,563
29		25	(h)	Chelsea	L	1-2	Hutchison	21,500
30	Mar	5	(a)	Arsenal	W	1-0	Hutchison	36,295
31		8	(a)	Newcastle U	L	0-2		34,595
32		11	(h)	Norwich C	D	2-2	Cottee 2	21,464
33		15	(a)	Southampton	D	1-1	Hutchison	15,178
34		18	(a)	Aston Villa	W	2-0	Moncur, Hutchison	28,682
35	Apr	8	(a)	Nottingham F	D	1-1	Dicks	28,361
36		13	(h)	Wimbledon	W	3-0	Dicks (pen), Boere, Cottee	21,804
37		17	(a)	Ipswich T	D	1-1	Boere	18,882
38		30	(h)	Blackburn R	W	2-0	Rieper, Hutchison	24,202
39	May	3	(h)	Queen's Park R	D	0-0		22,923
40		6	(a)	Crystal Palace	L	0-1		18,224
41		10	(h)	Liverpool	W	3-0	Holmes, Hutchison 2	22,446
42		14	(h)	Manchester U	D	1-1	Hughes	24,783

FINAL LEAGUE POSITION: 14th in F.A. Premier League

Appearances

Sub. Appearances

Goals

Miklosko	Breacker	Burrows	Potts	Martin	Allen	Bishop	Butler	Morley	Chapman	Holmes	Whitbread	Marsh	Moncur	Jones	Rowland	Hutchison	Cottee	Rush	Dicks	Brown	Hughes	Boere	Rieper	Williamson	Webster	
1	2	3	4*	5	6	7	8	9	10	11†	12	14														1
1	2	3	4	5	6	7	8*	9	10†	11	12	14														2
1	2	3	4	5	6	7			14		12	10*	8	9	11†											3
1	2	3	4	5	6*		8			11		10	7	12		9										4
1	2		4	5	6		8					10	7		3		9	11								5
1	2		4	5	6		8		12			10	7		3		9	11								6
1	2		4	5	6			8	11*			10	7		3	9		12								7
1	2		4	5	6			8				10	7		3	9		11								8
1	2		4	5	6			8*				10	7		3	11	9	12								9
1	2		4	5	6							10	7		3	8	9	11								10
1	2		4	5	6	7		8				10					9	11	3							11
1			4	5	6†	7*			12	14		10			2	8	9	11	3							12
1			4	5		6		8		2		10	7				9	11	3							13
1			4	5		6	8		10			2	7			10	9*	11	3	12						14
1			4	5		6	8	10				12	7				9	11	3	2						15
1			4			6*	8		11	5		10	7				9	12	3	2						16
1			4						6	7					5	9	8	3	2	11	10					17
1			4			6			11						7*	9	8	3	2	12	10	5				18
1	2		4	5	6			7							9	10	3		11	8						19
1	2	4*		5	6			7							9	8	3		11	10	12					20
1	2		4	5	8			7							9	12	3		11	10	6*					21
1	2		4	5	6			7		8†					9	12	3		11	10*	14					22
1	2		4			6		7*		8					9	12	3		11	10	5					23
1	2		4	5	12	6		14	7†			8			9		3	11*	10							24
1	2		4	5	12	6		7*		8					9		3	11†	10	14						25
1	2		4	5	6			7					8*	9	3		11	12		10						26
1			4	5	6			7					10	9	3	2	11*	12		8						27
1	2		4	5†	6			11*				7			10	9	3		12	14	8					28
1	2		4		6	11	8					7			10	9	3			5						29
1	2		4		6	11	8*					7			10	9	12	3		5						30
1	2		4		6	7	12								8	9	10*	3		11			5			31
1	2		4		6	8		7*							10	9	3		12	5	11					32
1	2		4		6	11		7							10	9	8*	3		12	5					33
1	2		4	6	8		11*				7	12		10†	9		3		14	5						34
1			4	6	8		7*	12							9		3	2	11	10	5					35
1	2		4	6	8			7							9		3		11	10	5					36
1	2		4	6*	8			11				7			12	9	3			10	5					37
1	2		4	6	8			11				7			9†		12	3		10*	5	14				38
1	2		4	6	8	12		11				7			9*		3			10†	5	14				39
1	2		4	6†	8	12		11				7			9*		3			10	5	14				40
1	2		4		6		9	7				8			10		3*		11		5	12				41
1	2		4	12	6		9	7				8			3	10*			11†		5	14				42
42	33	4	42	24	26	31	5	10	7	24	3	13	30	1	11	22	31	15	29	8	15	15	17	4		
					3			4	3		5	3	*	1	1	1	8		1	2	5	4		5		
					2	1			1		2					9	13	2	5		2	6	1			

1995-96

#	Month	Date		Opponent	Res	Score	Scorers	Att
1	Aug	19	(h)	Leeds U	L	1-2	Williamson	22,901
2		23	(a)	Manchester U	L	1-2	Bruce (og)	31,966
3		26	(a)	Nottingham F	D	1-1	Allen	26,645
4		30	(h)	Tottenham H	D	1-1	Hutchison	23,516
5	Sep	11	(h)	Chelsea	L	1-3	Hutchison	19,228
6		16	(a)	Arsenal	L	0-1		38,065
7		23	(h)	Everton	W	2-1	Dicks 2 (2 pens)	21,085
8	Oct	2	(a)	Southampton	D	0-0		13,568
9		16	(a)	Wimbledon	W	1-0	Cottee	9,411
10		21	(h)	Blackburn R	D	1-1	Dowie	21,776
11		28	(a)	Sheffield W	W	1-0	Dowie	23,917
12	Nov	4	(h)	Aston Villa	L	1-4	Dicks (pen)	23,637
13		18	(a)	Bolton W	W	3-0	Bishop, Cottee, Williamson	19,047
14		22	(h)	Liverpool	D	0-0		24,324
15		25	(h)	Queen's Park R	W	1-0	Cottee	21,504
16	Dec	2	(a)	Blackburn R	L	2-4	Dicks (pen), Slater	26,638
17		11	(a)	Everton	L	0-3		31,778
18		16	(h)	Southampton	W	2-1	Cottee, Dowie	18,501
19		23	(a)	Middlesbrough	L	2-4	Cottee, Dicks	28,640
20	Jan	1	(a)	Manchester C	L	1-2	Dowie	26,024
21		13	(a)	Leeds U	L	0-2		30,472
22		22	(h)	Manchester U	L	0-1		24,197
23		31	(h)	Coventry C	W	3-2	Rieper, Cottee, Dowie	18,884
24	Feb	3	(h)	Nottingham F	W	1-0	Slater	21,651
25		12	(a)	Tottenham H	W	1-0	Dani	29,781
26		17	(a)	Chelsea	W	2-1	Dicks, Williamson	25,252
27		21	(h)	Newcastle U	W	2-0	Williamson, Cottee	23,843
28		24	(h)	Arsenal	L	0-1		24,217
29	Mar	2	(a)	Coventry C	D	2-2	Cottee, Rieper	17,448
30		9	(h)	Middlesbrough	W	2-0	Dowie, Dicks (pen)	23,850
31		18	(a)	Newcastle U	L	0-3		36,331
32		23	(h)	Manchester C	W	4-2	Dowie 2, Dicks, Dani	24,017
33	Apr	6	(h)	Wimbledon	D	1-1	Dicks	20,462
34		8	(a)	Liverpool	L	0-2		40,326
35		13	(h)	Bolton W	W	1-0	Cottee	23,086
36		17	(a)	Aston Villa	D	1-1	Cottee	26,768
37		27	(a)	Queen's Park R	L	0-3		18,828
38	May	5	(h)	Sheffield W	D	1-1	Dicks	23,790

FINAL LEAGUE POSITION: 10th in F.A. Premier League

Appearances

Sub. Appearances

Goals

Miklosko	Breacker	Dicks	Potts	Rieper	Williamson	Moncur	Bishop	Cottee	Hutchison	Rowland	Martin	Boogers	Allen	Slater	Boere	Dowie	Lazaridis	Sealey	Hughes	Harkes	Finn	Brown	Whitbread	Lampard	Dani	Bilic	Gordon	Dumitrescu	Watson	Ferdinand	
1	2	3	4	5	6*	7	8	9	10	11†	12	13																			1
1	2	3	4	5	11*	7	8	9	10		12		6																		2
1	2	3	4	5		7	8	9*	10		12		6	11																	3
1	2	3	4	5		7	8	9	10*				6	11	12																4
1	2	3	4	5		7	6*	9	10					11		8	12														5
1	2	3	4	5		7°	6	9*	10†		12			11		8	13	14													6
1	2	3	4*	12	13	7	6	9†			5			11		8	10														7
1	2		4			7	6	12	10	3	5			11		9	8*														8
1		3	2	4		7	6	9			5		10	8			11														9
1		3	2	4		7	6	9	12		5		10*	8			11														10
1		3	2	4		7*	6	9	12		5		10†	8			11			13											11
1		3	2	4			6	9	10*		5	12	7†	8			11			13											12
1		2	4	10			6	9		3	5			8			11			7											13
1		2	4	10			6	9		3	5			8			11			7											14
1	12	2	4	10			6	9		3*	5		13	8			11			7†											15
1	2	3	4	5	10	6*	9°		12				14	13		8				7†											16
1	2	3	4	5	10	6	9*		12				7	8			11														17
1	12	3	2	4	10	7†	6	9			5*		13	8			11														18
1	2	3	4	5	10	7*	6	9	12				13	8			11†														19
	3	4	5	10*		7	6		12					8	9				11	2	1										20
1	6	2	5	4		7	8	9	3*				13	10			11														21
1		3	4	5	10	7	6	9	12				11*	8			2														22
1		3	4	5	10	7†	6	9*						8					11		2	12	13								23
1		3	4	5	10		6	9†						7*	8				11		2	12	13								24
1		3	2	5	10		6	12	11					8			7†							13	9*	4					25
1		3	2	5	10		6	12	11					8			7								9*	4					26
1		3	2	5	10		6	9†	11					8			7								12	4*		13			27
1		3	4	5	10		6	9	11					8			7					2*			12						28
1		3	2	5	10		6	9*	11					8			7								12	4					29
1	2	3	4		10		6	9*	11					8			7								5			12			30
	12	3	2	5	10		6*		11					8			7	1						13	4			9†			31
1	2	3		5	10		6		11					8			7							12	4			9*			32
1	2	3		5	10		6		11*				12	8			7								9	4					33
1	2	3		5	10		6	9	11					8			7*								12	4					34
1	2	3		5	10	12	6	9	13				7†	8			11*									4					35
1	2	3	4*	5	10	7		9	11					8											6			12			36
1	2	3	4	5	10	8*		9	11								7								6				12		37
1	2	3	4	5	10		9°	11†	12					8*			7							13	6					14	38
36	19	34	34	35	28	19	35	30	8	19	10	3	16	33	2	1	28	6	1	3		3	13	12	3	13		12			
	3		1	1	1		3	4	4	4	4		6	1		2	1			5			2	2	6		1	1	1	1	
		10		2	4		1	10	2		1	2		8									2								

1996-97

#	Month	Date		Opponent	Result		Scorers	Attendance
1	Aug	17	(a)	Arsenal	L	0-2		38,056
2		21	(h)	Coventry C	D	1-1	Rieper	21,580
3		24	(h)	Southampton	W	2-1	Hughes, Dicks (pen)	21,227
4	Sep	4	(a)	Middlesbrough	L	1-4	Hughes	30,061
5		8	(a)	Sunderland	D	0-0		18,581
6		14	(h)	Wimbledon	L	0-2		21,924
7		21	(a)	Nottingham F	W	2-0	Bowen, Hughes	23,352
8		29	(h)	Liverpool	L	1-2	Bilic	25,064
9	Oct	12	(a)	Everton	L	1-2	Dicks (pen)	36,541
10		19	(h)	Leicester C	W	1-0	Moncur	22,285
11		26	(h)	Blackburn R	W	2-1	Porfirio, Berg (og)	23,947
12	Nov	2	(a)	Tottenham H	L	0-1		32,975
13		16	(a)	Newcastle U	D	1-1	Rowland	36,552
14		23	(h)	Derby Co	D	1-1	Bishop	24,576
15		30	(a)	Sheffield W	D	0-0		22,321
16	Dec	4	(h)	Aston Villa	L	0-2		19,105
17		8	(h)	Manchester U	D	2-2	Raducioiu, Dicks (pen)	25,045
18		21	(a)	Chelsea	L	1-3	Porfirio	27,012
19		28	(h)	Sunderland	W	2-0	Bilic, Raducioiu	24,077
20	Jan	1	(h)	Nottingham F	L	0-1		22,358
21		11	(a)	Liverpool	D	0-0		40,102
22		20	(h)	Leeds U	L	0-2		19,441
23		29	(h)	Arsenal	L	1-2	Rose (og)	24,382
24	Feb	1	(a)	Blackburn R	L	1-2	Ferdinand	21,994
25		15	(a)	Derby Co	L	0-1		18,057
26		24	(h)	Tottenham H	W	4-3	Dicks 2 (1 pen), Kitson, Hartson	23,998
27	Mar	1	(a)	Leeds U	L	0-1		30,575
28		12	(h)	Chelsea	W	3-2	Dicks (pen), Kitson 2	24,502
29		15	(a)	Aston Villa	D	0-0		35,992
30		18	(a)	Wimbledon	D	1-1	Lazaridis	15,771
31		22	(a)	Coventry C	W	3-1	Hartson 2, Ferdinand	22,290
32	Apr	9	(h)	Middlesbrough	D	0-0		23,988
33		12	(a)	Southampton	L	0-2		15,245
34		19	(h)	Everton	D	2-2	Kitson 2	24,525
35		23	(a)	Leicester C	W	1-0	Moncur	20,327
36	May	3	(h)	Sheffield W	W	5-1	Kitson 3, Hartson 2	24,960
37		6	(h)	Newcastle U	D	0-0		24,617
38		11	(a)	Manchester U	L	0-2		55,249

FINAL LEAGUE POSITION: 14th in F.A. Premier League

Appearances

Sub. Appearances

Goals

Appearance and goalscoring chart (players across the top; match rows 1–38 down the right-hand side). Owing to the density of the grid, some cell-to-column alignments are approximate.

Miklosko	Breacker	Rowland	Rieper	Bilic	Dicks	Lampard	Dowie	Jones	Williamson	Hughes	Slater	Lazaridis	Ferdinand	Futre	Bowen	Raducioiu	Dumitrescu	Potts	Cottee	Moncur	Mautone	Bishop	Porfirio	Newell	Sealey	Hartson	Kitson	Omoyinmi	Hall	Lomas	Boylan	#
1	2	3†	4	5°	6	7*	8	9	10	11	12	13	14																			1
1	2*		4	5	3		8	9†	10	11	7	6		12	13																	2
1	12	4†	5	3			8		6	11	7*	9°	10		2	13	14															3
1	2		5	3	14	12	8			11	7†		10		6	9°	13	4*														4
1	2	13	4	5	3	12	8			11			14		10°	6	9*					7†										5
1	2*		4	5	3		8		7	11	12				10°	6	9†	14	13													6
	12		4	5	3	13	8			11			10		2	9*				7	1	6†										7
1	2		4	5	3		8			11		6†		12		9*	7					10	13									8
1		3		5	6		8			11			4	12	13	2*						10	7†	9								9
1	12		4	5	3		8			11		13			2*	9†	7	6				10										10
1	12		4	5	3	13	8			11	7		14					2*				10°	6	9†								11
1	2		4	5	3		8			11	7			12								10*	6	9								12
1	2	3		5	6		8			11				12		9*		4				10	7									13
1	2		5		3		8			11	7*			12				4				10	6	9								14
1	2	3	4	5	6	7	8			11*				12								10		9								15
1	2*	3†	4	5	6		8			11		13		12		9						10	7									16
1	11†		4	5*	3		8				7				2	13	9	12				10	6									17
1	3†		4	5	6	12			14	11					2		13			7°		8*	9	10								18
1			4	5	3	12			6	11					2		13			7*		8	9	10†								19
1			4	5	3	12		13	6	11					2°		7	14				8*	9	10†								20
1	2		4	5	3		8*		6†	11				12			13			10		7	9°	14								21
1	2		4	5	3		9		6	11	7*											8	12	10								22
1	2	3†	4	5	6	12	8			11		13								7*		10		9								23
	2	3*	4	5	6	7	8	9†		11		13		12								10			1							24
1	2	3†		5*	6		8			11		13		12				4		7		10				9						25
1	2	3		5	6					11	12							4		7		8				10	9*					26
1	2†	12		5	3		8			11		13			6*			4		7		10°	14				9					27
1	2			5	3		8			11	12†	13			6*			4		7°		10	14				9					28
1	2			5	3					11	12				6*			4		7		8				10	9					29
1	2		4	5	3		8			11*	12				6†					7		10				9	13					30
1	2*	12	4	5	3		8†			11°		13			6					7		10	14				9					31
1		3		5						11					7*			2				8	12			10	9		6	4		32
1	11*	3†		5							12	13						2		7		8°	14			10	9		6	4		33
1				5	3					11		13						2		7*		12	8†			10	9		6	4		34
1				5	3					11	12	13						2		7			8†			10	9*		6	4		35
1		12		5*	3					11†		13						2				8				10	9		6	4°	14	36
1		12		5	3					11		13						2		7†			8*			10	9		6	4		37
1†		12		5	3		8			11								2		7						10	9	15	6	4		38
36	22	11	26	35	31	3	18	5	13	31	2	13	11	4	15	6	3	17	2	26	1	26	15	6	1	11	14		7	7		
	4	4	2		10	5	3	2	2				1		9	4	5	2	5	4		3	1	1		3	8	1	1	1	1	
		1	1	2	6		3			1			2		1	2		2		1		2				5	8					

65

1997-98

1	Aug	9	(a)	Barnsley	W	2-1	Hartson, Lampard	18,667
2		13	(h)	Tottenham H	W	2-1	Hartson, Berkovic	25,354
3		23	(a)	Everton	L	1-2	Watson (og)	34,356
4		27	(a)	Coventry C	D	1-1	Kitson	18,291
5		30	(h)	Wimbledon	W	3-1	Hartson, Rieper, Berkovic	24,516
6	Sep	13	(a)	Manchester U	L	1-2	Hartson	55,068
7		20	(h)	Newcastle U	L	0-1		25,884
8		24	(a)	Arsenal	L	0-4		38,012
9		27	(h)	Liverpool	W	2-1	Hartson, Berkovic	25,908
10	Oct	4	(a)	Southampton	L	0-3		15,212
11		18	(h)	Bolton W	W	3-0	Berkovic, Hartson 2	24,864
12		27	(a)	Leicester C	L	1-2	Berkovic	20,201
13	Nov	9	(a)	Chelsea	L	1-2	Hartson (pen)	33,256
14		23	(a)	Leeds U	L	1-3	Lampard	29,447
15		29	(h)	Aston Villa	W	2-1	Hartson 2	24,976
16	Dec	3	(h)	Crystal Palace	W	4-1	Hartson, Berkovic, Unsworth, Lomas	23,335
17		6	(a)	Derby Co	L	0-2		29,300
18		13	(h)	Sheffield W	W	1-0	Kitson	24,344
19		20	(a)	Blackburn R	L	0-3		21,653
20		26	(h)	Coventry C	W	1-0	Kitson	22,477
21		28	(a)	Wimbledon	W	2-1	Kimble (og), Kitson	22,087
22	Jan	10	(h)	Barnsley	W	6-0	Lampard, Abou 2, Moncur, Hartson, Lazaridis	23,714
23		17	(a)	Tottenham H	L	0-1		30,284
24		31	(h)	Everton	D	2-2	Sinclair 2	25,905
25	Feb	7	(a)	Newcastle U	W	1-0	Lazaridis	36,736
26		21	(a)	Bolton W	D	1-1	Sinclair	25,000
27	Mar	2	(h)	Arsenal	D	0-0		25,717
28		11	(h)	Manchester U	D	1-1	Sinclair	25,892
29		14	(h)	Chelsea	W	2-1	Sinclair, Unsworth	25,829
30		30	(h)	Leeds U	W	3-0	Hartson, Abou, Pearce	24,107
31	Apr	4	(a)	Aston Villa	L	0-2		39,372
32		11	(h)	Derby Co	D	0-0		25,155
33		13	(a)	Sheffield W	D	1-1	Berkovic	28,036
34		18	(h)	Blackburn R	W	2-1	Hartson 2	24,733
35		25	(h)	Southampton	L	2-4	Sinclair, Lomas	25,878
36	May	2	(a)	Liverpool	L	0-5		44,414
37		5	(a)	Crystal Palace	D	3-3	Curcic (og), Omoyimni 2	19,129
38		10	(h)	Leicester C	W	4-3	Lampard, Abou 2, Sinclair	25,781

FINAL LEAGUE POSITION: 8th in F.A. Premier League

Appearances

Sub. Appearances

Goals

Miklosko	Breacker	Hughes	Potts	Ferdinand	Rieper	Moncur	Berkovic	Kitson	Hartson	Lomas	Lazaridis	Lampard	Terrier	Dowie	Unsworth	Pearce	Bishop	Impey	Moore	Forrest	Rowland	Abou	Alves	Hodges	Sinclair	Lama	Mean	Omoyimmi	
1	2*	3	4	5	6	7	8†	9°	10	11	12	13	14																1
1	2	12	4	5	6	7†	8	9*	10°	11	3	13		14															2
1	2°	12		5	6	7*	8†	9	10	11	3	13		14	4														3
1	2			5	6	7	8	9*	10	11	3			12	4														4
1	2			5	6	7	10		9	11	3			8	4														5
1	2	3	4	5		7*	8	9	10	11		12			6														6
1	2*	12	13	5			10†		9	11	3	7		8	4	6													7
1	2	12	5*						9	11	3	7		8	4	6	10												8
1	2		5				10		9	11		7		8	4	6		3											9
1	2		5				10		9	11				8*	4	6	7	3	12										10
		2		5		7	10	9	6	11				8	4					1	3								11
		2		5		7	10	9	6	11				8	4					1	3								12
		12		5		7†	10	9		11				8	4*	6	2			1	3	13							13
1	2			5		12	10*		9	11		7		13	4	6		3				8†							14
1	2		7	5			10		9	11					4	6		3				8*	12						15
	2			5		7	10		9	11	3*				4	6				1	12	8†	13						16
1	2*			5		7	10		9	11	3†			8	4	6						12	13						17
	12			5			8	9†	10	11		7			4	6		2*		1	3	13							18
				5			8	9*	10	11		7			4	6		2		1	3	12							19
		12		5			8*	9	10	11	3	7			4	6		2		1									20
	2			5				9	10	11	3			8	4	6		7		1									21
	2			5		12	10†	9			3			8	4	6		7*		1				13	11				22
	2			5		7	10†	9			3*		12	8	4	6				1				13	11				23
	2		4	5		7	10	9			3			8		6				1			12		11*				24
	2	12		5			8	9†	10		3	13			4	6		7*		1					11				25
				5		7	10	9			3			8	4	6		2		1					11				26
	2*	12		5		7	10	9			3			8	4	6									11	1			27
			4	5		7	10				3			8		6		2				9			11	1			28
		12		5		7	10				3			8	4	6		2*				9			11	1			29
	2			5		7	8*		10		3				4	6						9†			11	1	12	13	30
	2*			5		7		9	10		3			8	4	6									11	1			31
	12			5		7	10†	9			3	13		8	4	6*		2°							11	1	12		32
				5		7	10	9	11		3			8*	4	6		2								1	12		33
		12		5		7	10*	9	11		3				4	6		2							11	1			34
		4*		5		7	10		12		3			8		6		2				9				1			35
				5		7°	10*	9†			3			8	4	6		2				12			11	1	13	14	36
				5		7	10*	9			3			8*	4	6		2							11	1	12		37
				5		7	10*		9		3			8	4	6						9			11	1	12	2	38
13	18	2	14	35	5	17°	34	12	32	33	27	27		7	32	30	3	19		13	3	12			14	12		1	
1	3	9		3	1	1			1	4	1	5						1		1	7	4	2				3	4	
			1	1	7	4	15	2	2	4			2	1						5		7			2			2	

1973-74 SEASON

FIRST DIVISION

Leeds United	42	24	14	4	66	31	62
Liverpool	42	22	13	7	52	31	57
Derby County	42	17	14	11	52	42	48
Ipswich Town	42	18	11	13	67	58	47
Stoke City	42	15	16	11	54	42	46
Burnley	42	16	14	12	56	53	46
Everton	42	16	12	14	50	48	44
Queen's Pk. Rangers	42	13	17	12	56	52	43
Leicester City	42	13	16	13	51	41	42
Arsenal	42	14	14	14	49	51	42
Tottenham Hotspur	42	14	14	14	45	50	42
Wolverhampton Wns.	42	13	15	14	49	49	41
Sheffield United	42	14	12	16	44	49	40
Manchester City	42	14	12	16	39	46	40
Newcastle United	42	13	12	17	49	48	38
Coventry City	42	14	10	18	43	54	38
Chelsea	42	12	13	17	56	60	37
West Ham United	**42**	**11**	**15**	**16**	**55**	**60**	**37**
Birmingham City	42	12	13	17	52	64	37
Southampton	42	11	14	17	47	68	36
Manchester United	42	10	12	20	38	48	32
Norwich City	42	7	15	20	37	62	29

1974-75 SEASON

FIRST DIVISION

Derby County	42	21	11	10	67	49	53
Liverpool	42	20	11	11	60	39	51
Ipswich Town	42	23	5	14	66	44	51
Everton	42	16	18	8	56	42	50
Stoke City	42	17	15	10	64	48	49
Sheffield United	42	18	13	11	58	51	49
Middlesbrough	42	18	12	12	54	40	48
Manchester City	42	18	10	14	54	54	46
Leeds United	42	16	13	13	57	49	45
Burnley	42	17	11	14	68	67	45
Queen's Pk. Rangers	42	16	10	16	54	54	42
Wolverhampton Wns.	42	14	11	17	57	54	39
West Ham United	**42**	**13**	**13**	**16**	**58**	**59**	**39**
Coventry City	42	12	15	15	51	62	39
Newcastle United	42	15	9	18	59	72	39
Arsenal	42	13	11	18	47	49	37
Birmingham City	42	14	9	19	53	61	37
Leicester City	42	12	12	18	46	60	36
Tottenham Hotspur	42	13	8	21	52	63	34
Luton Town	42	11	11	20	47	65	33
Chelsea	42	9	15	18	42	72	33
Carlisle United	42	12	5	25	43	59	29

1975-76 SEASON

FIRST DIVISION

Liverpool	42	23	14	5	66	31	60
Queen's Pk. Rangers	42	24	11	7	67	33	59
Manchester United	42	23	10	10	68	42	56
Derby County	42	21	11	10	75	58	53
Leeds United	42	21	9	12	65	46	51
Ipswich Town	42	16	14	12	54	48	46
Leicester City	42	13	19	10	48	51	45
Manchester City	42	16	12	15	64	46	43
Tottenham Hotspur	42	14	15	13	63	63	43
Norwich City	42	16	10	16	58	58	42
Everton	42	15	12	15	60	66	42
Stoke City	42	15	11	16	48	50	41
Middlesbrough	42	15	10	17	46	45	40
Coventry City	42	13	14	15	47	57	40
Newcastle United	42	15	9	18	71	62	39
Aston Villa	42	11	17	14	51	59	39
Arsenal	42	13	10	19	47	53	36
West Ham United	**42**	**13**	**10**	**19**	**48**	**71**	**36**
Birmingham City	42	13	7	22	57	75	33
Wolverhampton Wns.	42	10	10	22	51	68	30
Burnley	42	9	10	23	43	66	28
Sheffield United	42	6	10	26	33	82	22

1976-77 SEASON

FIRST DIVISION

Liverpool	42	23	11	8	62	33	57
Manchester City	42	21	14	7	60	34	56
Ipswich Town	42	22	8	12	66	39	52
Aston Villa	42	22	7	13	76	50	51
Newcastle United	42	18	13	11	64	49	49
Manchester United	42	18	11	13	71	62	47
West Brom. Albion	42	16	13	13	62	56	45
Arsenal	42	16	11	15	64	59	43
Everton	42	14	14	14	62	64	42
Leeds United	42	15	12	15	48	51	42
Leicester City	42	12	18	12	47	60	42
Middlesbrough	42	14	13	15	40	45	41
Birmingham City	42	13	12	17	63	61	38
Queen's Pk. Rangers	42	13	12	17	47	52	38
Derby County	42	9	19	14	50	55	37
Norwich City	42	14	9	19	47	64	37
West Ham United	**42**	**11**	**14**	**17**	**46**	**65**	**36**
Bristol City	42	11	13	18	38	48	35
Coventry City	42	10	15	17	48	59	35
Sunderland	42	11	12	19	46	54	34
Stoke City	42	10	14	18	28	51	34
Tottenham Hotspur	42	12	9	21	48	72	33

1977-78 SEASON

FIRST DIVISION

Nottingham Forest	42	25	14	3	69	24	64
Liverpool	42	24	9	9	65	34	57
Everton	42	22	11	9	76	45	55
Manchester City	42	20	12	10	74	51	52
Arsenal	42	21	10	11	60	37	52
West Brom. Albion	42	18	14	10	62	53	50
Coventry City	42	18	12	12	75	62	48
Aston Villa	42	18	10	14	57	42	46
Leeds United	42	18	10	14	63	53	46
Manchester United	42	16	10	16	67	63	42
Birmingham City	42	16	9	17	55	60	41
Derby County	42	14	13	15	54	59	41
Norwich City	42	11	18	13	52	66	40
Middlesbrough	42	12	15	15	42	54	39
Wolverhampton Wns.	42	12	12	18	51	64	36
Chelsea	42	11	14	17	46	69	36
Bristol City	42	11	13	18	49	53	35
Ipswich Town	42	11	13	18	47	61	35
Queen's Pk. Rangers	42	9	15	18	47	64	33
West Ham United	**42**	**12**	**8**	**22**	**52**	**69**	**32**
Newcastle United	42	6	10	26	42	78	22
Leicester City	42	5	12	25	26	70	22

1978-79 SEASON

SECOND DIVISION

Crystal Palace	42	19	19	4	51	24	57
Brighton & Hove Alb.	42	23	10	9	72	39	56
Stoke City	42	20	16	6	58	31	56
Sunderland	42	22	11	9	70	44	55
West Ham United	**42**	**18**	**14**	**10**	**70**	**39**	**50**
Notts County	42	14	16	12	48	60	44
Preston North End	42	12	18	12	59	57	42
Newcastle United	42	17	8	17	51	55	42
Cardiff City	42	16	10	16	56	70	42
Fulham	42	13	15	14	50	47	41
Orient	42	15	10	17	51	51	40
Cambridge United	42	12	16	14	44	52	40
Burnley	42	14	12	16	51	62	40
Oldham Athletic	42	13	13	16	52	61	39
Wrexham	42	12	14	16	45	42	38
Bristol Rovers	42	14	10	18	48	60	38
Leicester City	42	10	17	15	43	52	37
Luton Town	42	13	10	19	60	57	36
Charlton Athletic	42	11	13	18	60	69	35
Sheffield United	42	11	12	19	52	69	34
Millwall	42	11	10	21	42	61	32
Blackburn Rovers	42	10	10	22	41	72	30

1979-80 SEASON

SECOND DIVISION

Leicester City	42	21	13	8	58	38	55
Sunderland	42	21	12	9	69	42	54
Birmingham City	42	21	11	10	58	38	53
Chelsea	42	23	7	12	66	52	53
Queen's Pk. Rangers	42	18	13	11	75	53	49
Luton Town	42	16	17	9	66	45	49
West Ham United	**42**	**20**	**7**	**15**	**54**	**43**	**47**
Cambridge United	42	14	16	12	61	53	44
Newcastle United	42	15	14	13	53	49	44
Preston North End	42	12	19	11	56	52	43
Oldham Athletic	42	16	11	15	49	53	43
Swansea City	42	17	9	16	48	53	43
Shrewsbury Town	42	18	5	19	60	53	41
Orient	42	12	17	13	48	54	41
Cardiff City	42	16	8	18	41	48	40
Wrexham	42	16	6	20	40	49	38
Notts County	42	11	15	16	51	52	37
Watford	42	12	13	17	39	46	37
Bristol Rovers	42	11	13	18	50	64	35
Fulham	42	11	7	24	42	74	29
Burnley	42	6	15	21	39	73	27
Charlton Athletic	42	6	10	26	39	78	22

1980-81 SEASON

SECOND DIVISION

West Ham United	**42**	**28**	**10**	**4**	**79**	**29**	**66**
Notts County	42	18	17	7	49	38	53
Swansea City	42	18	14	10	64	44	50
Blackburn Rovers	42	16	18	8	42	29	50
Luton Town	42	18	12	12	61	46	48
Derby County	42	15	15	12	57	52	45
Grimsby Town	42	15	15	12	44	42	45
Queen's Pk. Rangers	42	15	13	14	56	46	43
Watford	42	16	11	15	50	45	43
Sheffield Wednesday	42	17	8	17	53	51	42
Newcastle United	42	14	14	14	30	45	42
Chelsea	42	14	12	16	46	41	40
Cambridge United	42	17	6	17	53	65	40
Shrewsbury Town	42	11	17	14	46	47	39
Oldham Athletic	42	12	15	15	39	48	39
Wrexham	42	12	14	16	43	45	38
Orient	42	13	12	17	52	56	38
Bolton Wanderers	42	14	10	18	61	66	38
Cardiff City	42	12	12	18	44	60	36
Preston North End	42	11	14	17	41	62	36
Bristol City	42	7	16	19	29	51	30
Bristol Rovers	42	5	13	24	34	65	23

1981-82 SEASON

FIRST DIVISION

Liverpool	42	26	9	7	80	32	87
Ipswich Town	42	26	5	11	75	53	83
Manchester United	42	22	12	8	59	29	78
Tottenham Hotspur	42	20	11	11	67	48	71
Arsenal	42	20	11	11	48	37	71
Swansea City	42	21	6	15	58	51	69
Southampton	42	19	9	14	72	67	66
Everton	42	17	13	12	56	50	64
West Ham United	**42**	**14**	**16**	**12**	**66**	**57**	**58**
Manchester City	42	15	13	14	49	50	58
Aston Villa	42	15	12	15	55	53	57
Nottingham Forest	42	15	12	15	42	48	57
Brighton & Hove Alb.	42	13	13	16	43	52	52
Coventry City	42	13	11	18	56	62	50
Notts County	42	13	8	21	45	69	47
Birmingham City	42	10	14	18	53	61	44
West Brom. Albion	42	11	11	20	46	57	44
Stoke City	42	12	8	22	44	63	44
Sunderland	42	11	11	20	38	58	44
Leeds United	42	10	12	20	39	61	42
Wolverhampton Wns.	42	10	10	22	32	63	40
Middlesbrough	42	8	15	19	34	52	39

1982-83 SEASON

FIRST DIVISION

Liverpool	42	24	10	8	87	37	82
Watford	42	22	5	15	74	57	71
Manchester United	42	19	13	8	56	38	70
Tottenham Hotspur	42	20	9	13	65	50	69
Nottingham Forest	42	20	9	13	62	50	69
Aston Villa	42	21	5	16	62	50	68
Everton	42	18	10	14	66	48	64
West Ham United	**42**	**20**	**4**	**18**	**68**	**62**	**64**
Ipswich Town	42	15	13	14	64	50	58
Arsenal	42	16	10	16	58	56	58
West Brom. Albion	42	15	12	15	51	49	57
Southampton	42	15	12	15	54	58	57
Stoke City	42	16	9	17	53	64	57
Norwich City	42	14	12	16	52	58	54
Notts County	42	15	7	21	55	71	52
Sunderland	42	12	14	16	48	61	50
Birmingham City	42	12	15	16	40	55	50
Luton Town	42	12	13	17	65	84	49
Coventry City	42	13	9	20	48	59	48
Manchester City	42	13	8	21	47	70	47
Swansea City	42	10	11	21	51	69	41
Brighton & Hove Alb.	42	9	13	20	38	67	40

1983-84 SEASON

FIRST DIVISION

Liverpool	42	22	14	6	73	32	80
Southampton	42	22	11	9	66	38	77
Nottingham Forest	42	22	8	12	76	45	74
Manchester United	42	20	14	8	71	41	74
Queen's Pk. Rangers	42	22	7	13	67	37	73
Arsenal	42	18	9	15	74	60	63
Everton	42	16	14	12	44	42	62
Tottenham Hotspur	42	17	10	15	64	65	61
West Ham United	**42**	**17**	**9**	**16**	**60**	**55**	**60**
Aston Villa	42	17	9	16	59	61	60
Watford	42	16	9	17	68	77	57
Ipswich Town	42	15	8	19	55	57	53
Sunderland	42	13	13	16	42	53	52
Norwich City	42	12	15	15	48	49	51
Leicester City	42	13	12	17	65	68	51
Luton Town	42	14	9	19	53	66	51
West Brom. Albion	42	14	9	19	48	62	51
Stoke City	42	13	11	18	44	63	50
Coventry City	42	13	11	18	57	77	50
Birmingham City	42	12	12	18	39	50	48
Notts County	42	10	11	21	50	72	41
Wolverhampton Wns.	42	6	11	25	27	80	29

1984-85 SEASON

FIRST DIVISION

Everton	42	28	6	8	88	43	90
Liverpool	42	22	11	9	78	35	77
Tottenham Hotspur	42	23	8	11	78	51	77
Manchester United	42	22	10	10	77	47	76
Southampton	42	19	11	12	56	47	68
Chelsea	42	18	12	12	63	48	66
Arsenal	42	19	9	14	61	49	66
Sheffield Wednesday	42	17	14	11	58	45	65
Nottingham Forest	42	19	7	16	56	48	64
Aston Villa	42	15	11	16	60	60	56
Watford	42	14	13	15	81	71	55
West Brom. Albion	42	16	7	19	58	62	55
Luton Town	42	15	9	18	57	61	54
Newcastle United	42	13	13	16	55	70	52
Leicester City	42	15	6	21	65	73	51
West Ham United	**42**	**13**	**12**	**17**	**51**	**68**	**51**
Ipswich Town	42	13	11	18	46	57	50
Coventry City	42	15	5	22	47	64	50
Queen's Pk. Rangers	42	13	11	18	53	72	50
Norwich City	42	13	10	19	46	64	49
Sunderland	42	10	10	22	40	62	40
Stoke City	42	3	8	31	24	91	17

1985-86 SEASON

FIRST DIVISION

Liverpool	42	26	10	6	89	37	88
Everton	42	26	8	8	87	41	86
West Ham United	**42**	**26**	**6**	**10**	**74**	**40**	**84**
Manchester United	42	22	10	10	70	36	76
Sheffield Wednesday	42	21	10	11	63	54	73
Chelsea	42	20	11	11	57	56	71
Arsenal	42	20	9	13	49	47	69
Nottingham Forest	42	19	11	12	69	53	68
Luton Town	42	18	12	12	61	44	66
Tottenham Hotspur	42	19	8	15	74	52	65
Newcastle United	42	17	12	13	67	72	63
Watford	42	16	11	15	69	62	59
Queen's Pk. Rangers	42	15	7	20	53	64	52
Southampton	42	12	10	20	51	62	46
Manchester City	42	11	12	19	43	57	45
Aston Villa	42	10	14	18	51	67	44
Coventry City	42	11	10	21	48	71	43
Oxford United	42	10	12	20	62	80	42
Leicester City	42	10	12	20	54	76	42
Ipswich Town	42	11	8	23	32	55	41
Birmingham City	42	8	5	29	30	73	29
West Brom. Albion	42	4	12	26	35	89	24

1986-87 SEASON

FIRST DIVISION

Everton	42	26	8	8	76	31	86
Liverpool	42	23	8	11	72	42	77
Tottenham Hotspur	42	21	8	13	68	43	71
Arsenal	42	20	10	12	58	35	70
Norwich City	42	17	17	8	53	51	68
Wimbledon	42	19	9	14	57	50	66
Luton Town	42	18	12	12	47	45	66
Nottingham Forest	42	18	11	13	64	51	65
Watford	42	18	9	15	67	54	63
Coventry City	42	17	12	13	50	45	63
Manchester United	42	14	14	14	52	45	56
Southampton	42	14	10	18	69	68	52
Sheffield Wednesday	42	13	13	16	58	59	52
Chelsea	42	13	13	16	53	64	52
West Ham United	**42**	**14**	**10**	**18**	**52**	**67**	**52**
Queen's Pk. Rangers	42	13	11	18	48	64	50
Newcastle United	42	12	11	19	47	65	47
Oxford United	42	11	13	18	44	69	46
Charlton Athletic	42	11	11	20	45	55	44
Leicester City	42	11	9	22	54	76	42
Manchester City	42	8	15	19	36	57	39
Aston Villa	42	8	12	22	45	79	36

1987-88 SEASON

FIRST DIVISION

Liverpool	40	26	12	2	87	24	90
Manchester United	40	23	12	5	71	38	81
Nottingham Forest	40	20	13	7	67	39	73
Everton	40	19	13	8	53	27	70
Queen's Pk. Rangers	40	19	10	11	48	38	67
Arsenal	40	18	12	10	58	39	66
Wimbledon	40	14	15	11	58	47	57
Newcastle United	40	14	14	12	55	53	56
Luton Town	40	14	11	15	57	58	53
Coventry City	40	13	14	13	46	53	53
Sheffield Wednesday	40	15	8	17	52	66	53
Southampton	40	12	14	14	49	53	50
Tottenham Hotspur	40	12	11	17	38	48	47
Norwich City	40	12	9	19	40	52	45
Derby County	40	10	13	17	35	45	43
West Ham United	**40**	**9**	**15**	**16**	**40**	**52**	**42**
Charlton Athletic	40	9	15	16	38	52	42
Chelsea	40	9	15	16	50	68	42
Portsmouth	40	7	14	19	36	66	35
Watford	40	7	11	22	27	51	32
Oxford United	40	6	13	21	44	80	31

1988-89 SEASON

FIRST DIVISION

Arsenal	38	22	10	6	73	36	76
Liverpool	38	22	10	6	65	28	76
Nottingham Forest	38	17	13	8	64	43	64
Norwich City	38	17	11	10	48	45	62
Derby County	38	17	7	14	40	38	58
Tottenham Hotspur	38	15	12	11	60	46	57
Coventry City	38	14	13	11	47	42	55
Everton	38	14	12	12	50	45	54
Queen's Pk. Rangers	38	14	11	13	43	37	53
Millwall	38	14	11	13	47	52	53
Manchester United	38	13	12	13	45	35	51
Wimbledon	38	14	9	15	50	46	51
Southampton	38	10	15	13	52	66	45
Charlton Athletic	38	10	12	16	44	58	42
Sheffield Wednesday	38	10	12	16	34	51	42
Luton Town	38	10	11	17	42	52	41
Aston Villa	38	9	13	16	45	56	40
Middlesbrough	38	9	12	17	44	61	39
West Ham United	**38**	**10**	**8**	**20**	**37**	**62**	**38**
Newcastle United	38	7	10	21	32	63	31

1989-90 SEASON

SECOND DIVISION

Leeds United	46	24	13	9	79	52	85
Sheffield United	46	24	13	9	78	58	85
Newcastle United	46	22	14	10	80	55	80
Swindon Town	46	20	14	12	79	59	74
Blackburn Rovers	46	19	17	10	74	59	74
Sunderland	46	20	14	12	70	64	74
West Ham United	**46**	**20**	**12**	**14**	**80**	**57**	**72**
Oldham Athletic	46	19	14	13	70	57	71
Ipswich Town	46	19	12	15	67	66	69
Wolverhampton Wns.	46	18	13	15	67	60	67
Port Vale	46	15	16	15	62	57	61
Portsmouth	46	15	16	15	62	65	61
Leicester City	46	15	14	17	67	79	59
Hull City	46	14	16	16	58	65	58
Watford	46	14	15	17	58	60	57
Plymouth Argyle	46	14	13	19	58	63	55
Oxford United	46	15	9	22	57	66	54
Brighton & Hove Alb.	46	15	9	22	56	72	54
Barnsley	46	13	15	18	49	71	54
West Brom. Albion	46	12	15	19	67	71	51
Middlesbrough	46	13	11	22	52	63	50
Bournemouth	46	12	12	22	57	76	48
Bradford City	46	9	14	23	44	68	41
Stoke City	46	6	19	21	35	63	37

1990-91 SEASON

SECOND DIVISION

Oldham Athletic	46	25	13	8	83	53	88
West Ham United	**46**	**24**	**15**	**7**	**60**	**34**	**87**
Sheffield Wednesday	46	22	16	8	80	51	82
Notts County	46	23	11	12	76	55	80
Millwall	46	20	13	13	70	51	73
Brighton & Hove Alb.	46	21	7	18	63	69	70
Middlesbrough	46	20	9	17	66	47	69
Barnsley	46	19	12	15	63	48	69
Bristol City	46	20	7	19	68	71	67
Oxford United	46	14	19	13	69	66	61
Newcastle United	46	14	17	15	49	56	59
Wolverhampton Wns.	46	13	19	14	63	63	58
Bristol Rovers	46	15	13	18	56	59	58
Ipswich Town	46	13	18	15	60	68	57
Port Vale	46	15	12	19	56	64	57
Charlton Athletic	46	13	17	16	57	61	56
Portsmouth	46	14	11	21	58	70	53
Plymouth Argyle	46	12	17	17	54	68	53
Blackburn Rovers	46	14	10	22	51	66	52
Watford	46	12	15	19	45	59	51
Swindon Town	46	12	14	20	65	73	50
Leicester City	46	14	8	24	60	83	50
West Brom. Albion	46	10	18	18	52	61	48
Hull City	46	10	15	21	57	85	45

1991-92 SEASON

FIRST DIVISION

Leeds United	42	22	16	4	74	37	82
Manchester United	42	21	15	6	63	33	78
Sheffield Wednesday	42	21	12	9	62	49	75
Arsenal	42	19	15	8	81	46	72
Manchester City	42	20	10	12	61	48	70
Liverpool	42	16	16	10	47	40	64
Aston Villa	42	17	9	16	48	44	60
Nottingham Forest	42	16	11	15	60	58	59
Sheffield United	42	16	9	17	65	63	57
Crystal Palace	42	14	15	13	53	61	57
Queen's Pk. Rangers	42	12	18	12	48	47	54
Everton	42	13	14	15	52	51	53
Wimbledon	42	13	14	15	53	53	53
Chelsea	42	13	14	15	50	60	53
Tottenham	42	15	7	20	58	63	52
Southampton	42	14	10	18	39	55	52
Oldham Athletic	42	14	9	19	63	67	51
Norwich City	42	11	12	19	47	63	45
Coventry City	42	11	11	20	35	44	44
Luton Town	42	10	12	20	38	71	42
Notts County	42	10	10	22	40	62	40
West Ham United	**42**	**9**	**11**	**22**	**37**	**59**	**38**

1992-93 SEASON

FIRST DIVISION

Newcastle United	46	29	9	8	92	38	96
West Ham United	**46**	**26**	**10**	**10**	**81**	**41**	**88**
Portsmouth	46	26	10	10	80	46	88
Tranmere Rovers	46	23	10	13	72	56	79
Swindon Town	46	21	13	12	74	59	76
Leicester City	46	22	10	14	71	64	76
Millwall	46	18	16	12	65	53	70
Derby County	46	19	9	18	68	57	66
Grimsby Town	46	19	7	20	58	57	64
Peterborough United	46	16	14	16	55	63	62
Wolverhampton Wns.	46	16	13	17	57	56	61
Charlton Athletic	46	16	13	17	49	46	61
Barnsley	46	17	9	20	56	60	60
Oxford United	46	14	14	18	53	56	56
Bristol City	46	14	14	18	49	67	56
Watford	46	14	13	19	57	71	55
Notts County	46	12	16	18	55	70	52
Southend United	46	13	13	20	54	64	52
Birmingham City	46	13	12	21	50	72	51
Luton Town	46	10	21	15	48	62	51
Sunderland	46	13	11	22	50	64	50
Brentford	46	13	10	23	52	71	49
Cambridge United	46	11	16	19	48	69	49
Bristol Rovers	46	10	11	25	55	87	41

1993-94 SEASON

F.A. PREMIER LEAGUE

Manchester United	42	27	11	4	80	38	92
Blackburn Rovers	42	25	9	8	63	36	84
Newcastle United	42	23	8	11	82	41	77
Arsenal	42	18	17	7	53	28	71
Leeds United	42	18	16	8	65	39	70
Wimbledon	42	18	11	13	56	53	65
Sheffield Wednesday	42	16	16	10	76	54	64
Liverpool	42	17	9	16	59	55	60
Queen's Pk. Rangers	42	16	12	14	62	64	60
Aston Villa	42	15	12	15	46	50	57
Coventry City	42	14	14	14	43	45	56
Norwich City	42	12	17	13	65	61	53
West Ham United	**42**	**13**	**13**	**16**	**47**	**58**	**52**
Chelsea	42	13	12	17	49	53	51
Tottenham Hotspur	42	11	12	19	54	59	45
Manchester City	42	9	18	15	38	49	45
Everton	42	12	8	22	42	63	44
Southampton	42	12	7	23	49	66	43
Ipswich Town	42	9	16	17	35	58	43
Sheffield United	42	8	18	16	42	60	42
Oldham Athletic	42	9	13	20	42	68	40
Swindon Town	42	5	15	22	47	100	30

1994-95 SEASON

F.A. PREMIER LEAGUE

Blackburn Rovers	42	27	8	7	80	39	89
Manchester United	42	26	10	6	77	28	88
Nottingham Forest	42	22	11	9	72	43	77
Liverpool	42	21	11	10	65	37	74
Leeds United	42	20	13	9	59	38	63
Newcastle United	42	20	12	10	67	47	72
Tottenham Hotspur	42	16	14	12	66	58	62
Queen's Pk. Rangers	42	17	9	16	61	59	60
Wimbledon	42	15	11	16	48	65	56
Southampton	42	12	18	12	61	63	54
Chelsea	42	13	15	14	50	55	54
Arsenal	42	13	12	17	52	49	51
Sheffield Wednesday	42	13	12	17	49	57	51
West Ham United	**42**	**13**	**11**	**18**	**44**	**48**	**50**
Everton	42	11	17	14	44	51	50
Coventry City	42	12	14	16	44	62	50
Manchester City	42	12	13	17	53	64	49
Aston Villa	42	11	15	16	51	56	48
Crystal Palace	42	11	12	19	34	49	45
Norwich City	42	10	13	19	37	54	43
Leicester City	42	6	11	25	45	80	29
Ipswich Town	42	7	6	29	36	93	27

1995-96 SEASON

F.A. PREMIER LEAGUE

Manchester United	38	25	7	6	73	35	82
Newcastle United	38	24	6	8	66	37	78
Liverpool	38	20	11	7	70	34	71
Aston Villa	38	18	9	11	52	35	63
Arsenal	38	17	12	9	49	32	63
Everton	38	17	10	11	64	44	61
Blackburn Rovers	38	18	7	13	61	47	61
Tottenham Hotspur	38	16	13	9	50	38	61
Nottingham Forest	38	15	13	10	50	54	58
West Ham United	**38**	**14**	**9**	**15**	**43**	**52**	**51**
Chelsea	38	12	14	12	46	44	50
Middlesbrough	38	11	10	17	35	50	43
Leeds United	38	12	7	19	40	57	43
Wimbledon	38	10	11	17	55	70	41
Sheffield Wednesday	38	10	10	18	48	61	40
Coventry City	38	8	14	16	42	60	38
Southampton	38	9	11	18	34	52	38
Manchester City	38	9	11	18	33	58	38
Queen's Park Rangers	38	9	6	23	38	57	33
Bolton Wanderers	38	8	5	25	39	71	29

1996-97 SEASON

F.A. PREMIER LEAGUE

Manchester United	38	21	12	5	76	44	75
Newcastle United	38	19	11	8	73	40	68
Arsenal	38	19	11	8	62	32	68
Liverpool	38	19	11	8	62	37	68
Aston Villa	38	17	10	11	47	34	61
Chelsea	38	16	11	11	58	55	59
Sheffield Wednesday	38	14	15	9	50	51	57
Wimbledon	38	15	11	12	49	46	56
Leicester City	38	12	11	15	46	54	47
Tottenham Hotspur	38	13	7	18	44	51	46
Leeds United	38	11	13	14	28	38	46
Derby County	38	11	13	14	45	58	46
Blackburn Rovers	38	9	15	14	42	43	42
West Ham United	**38**	**10**	**12**	**16**	**39**	**48**	**42**
Everton	38	10	12	16	44	57	42
Southampton	38	10	11	17	50	56	41
Coventry City	38	9	14	15	38	54	41
Sunderland	38	10	10	18	35	53	40
Middlesbrough	38	10	12	16	51	60	39
Nottingham Forest	38	6	16	16	31	59	34

1997-98 SEASON

F.A. PREMIER LEAGUE

Arsenal	38	23	9	6	68	33	78
Manchester United	38	23	8	7	73	26	77
Liverpool	38	18	11	9	68	42	65
Chelsea	38	20	3	15	71	43	63
Leeds United	38	17	8	13	57	46	59
Blackburn Rovers	38	16	10	12	57	52	58
Aston Villa	38	17	6	15	49	48	57
West Ham United	**38**	**16**	**8**	**14**	**56**	**57**	**56**
Derby County	38	16	7	15	52	49	55
Leicester City	38	13	14	11	51	41	53
Coventry City	38	12	16	10	46	44	52
Southampton	38	14	6	18	50	55	48
Newcastle United	38	11	11	16	35	44	44
Tottenham Hotspur	38	11	11	16	44	56	44
Wimbledon	38	10	14	14	34	46	44
Sheffield Wednesday	38	12	8	18	52	67	44
Everton	38	9	13	16	41	56	40
Bolton Wanderers	38	9	13	16	41	61	40
Barnsley	38	10	5	23	37	82	35
Crystal Palace	38	8	9	21	37	71	33